STUDENT
HACKS

An Hachette UK Company
www.hachette.co.uk

Summersdale Publishers Ltd
Part of Octopus Publishing Group Limited
Carmelite House
50 Victoria Embankment
LONDON
EC4Y 0DZ
UK

www.summersdale.com

Printed and bound in Croatia

ISBN: 978-1-78685-246-5

Substantial discounts on bulk quantities of Summersdale books are available to corporations,
professional associations and other organisations. For details contact general enquiries:
telephone: +44 (0) 1243 771107 or email: enquiries@summersdale.com.

STUDENT HACKS

Handy Hints to Make Uni Life Easier

Standard cracked phone screen

Toilet roll/alarm-clock amplifier

Drawing pins for stability

Dan Marshall

Over **130** amazing hacks inside!

summersdale

DISCLAIMER

Neither the author nor the publisher can be held responsible for any loss or claim arising out of the use, or misuse, of the suggestions made herein.

CONTENTS

INTRODUCTION

Welcome to the world of being a student! Where gaining knowledge is top priority and partying follows closely behind. The majority of your time at uni will be spent moaning about lectures, then about exams and assignments, and then about how skint you are every month. But don't worry, you're guaranteed to have the best, most fulfilling time of your life. And to prevent you from moaning too much, this nifty book will be your go-to for many of your being-responsible-and-mature needs. With low-budget tips and tricks on all aspects of student living, from turning your laptop bag into a rucksack to opening a bottle of wine without a corkscrew, you'll go from fresher to know-it-all before your first semester even begins.

ESSENTIAL STUDENT HACKS

Are you always forgetting your timetable and what room your lecture is in? Is changing the sheets a massive chore that takes double the time it should? This chapter offers you the most essential hacks around to help you survive in style.

ALARM-CLOCK AMPLIFIER

Is your alarm just that bit too quiet to wake you from your peaceful slumber whenever you have to be up for uni? Make sure you never sleep in again with this hack.

Cut a slot in a toilet roll tube big enough to fit your phone, and stop the roll from rolling away by sticking some drawing pins into the tube to act as feet. As well as creating a docking station, you've also created an amplifier (this can be used when you want to play loud music too).

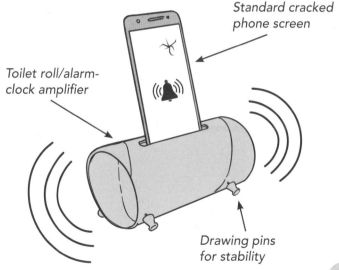

Standard cracked phone screen

Toilet roll/alarm-clock amplifier

Drawing pins for stability

SCHEDULE SCHEDULER

Never miss a class with this hack. When you receive your timetable for the year, screenshot it and save it as your background photo on your phone. If you're in bed and you've forgotten if you need to attend a lecture, all you have to do is stretch across and you'll have the answer right at your fingertips.

Just-visible timetable

Standard cracked phone screen

7:30

Day	Subject	Time	Room
Mon	English literature	09.00	B21
Tues	Psychology	11.00	A13
Weds	English language	10.00	B18
Thurs	History	09.00	C12
Fri	English literature	10.00	B21

slide to unlock

CHANGING THE DUVET COVER

Sick of wasting time trying to change your bed sheets? You need this hack.

Turn the duvet cover inside out, with the open side at the bottom of the bed, and spread it out on your mattress. Place the duvet on top and make sure all the corners are aligned. Starting at the top, roll the cover and duvet up, like you would a Swiss roll. Once you've rolled them, flip the duvet cover over one end of the 'Swiss roll' to expose the correct side of it. Then repeat on the other side, and then in the middle. Now unroll your bedding to reveal a beautifully made bed.

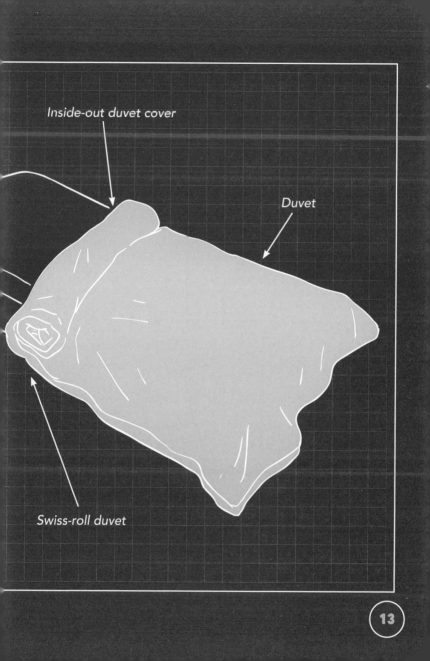

Inside-out duvet cover

Duvet

Swiss-roll duvet

EASY-PEASY GROCERY LIST

You're a student. Your memory should be good. At least that's what you think until you get to the supermarket without a list and then you have to bumble through the aisles wondering what you need.

Save yourself from looking like a lemon in the lemon aisle by taking a photo of your fridge and freezer compartments to remind yourself of what you've run out of.

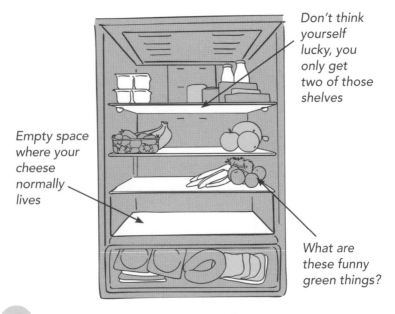

Don't think yourself lucky, you only get two of those shelves

Empty space where your cheese normally lives

What are these funny green things?

LAPTOP BACKPACK

Does your laptop turn into the biggest first-world problem when you have to lug it to class every day? Say goodbye to the achy shoulder and lop-sided walk with this helpful hack.

Extend the strap on your laptop case to maximum length then unclasp one of the ends. Feed it through the handle of the laptop case then clasp the strap back in its original place. Hold the bag by the two ends of the strap and put it on your back like you would a rucksack. Happy days!

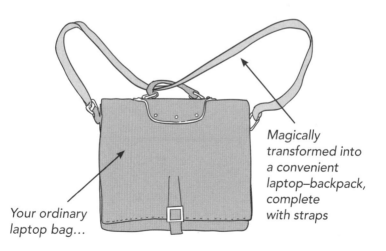

Magically transformed into a convenient laptop–backpack, complete with straps

Your ordinary laptop bag...

MICROWAVE SPACE MAXIMISER

Microwaves save the day (but mainly time) when you want to quickly whip something up. But if you want to cook more than one item you usually have to do them separately, which then doubles the cooking time.

To solve this issue, decant your food into two bowls and place the second bowl in the microwave on top of a mug. Voila! Your food is ready in half the time.

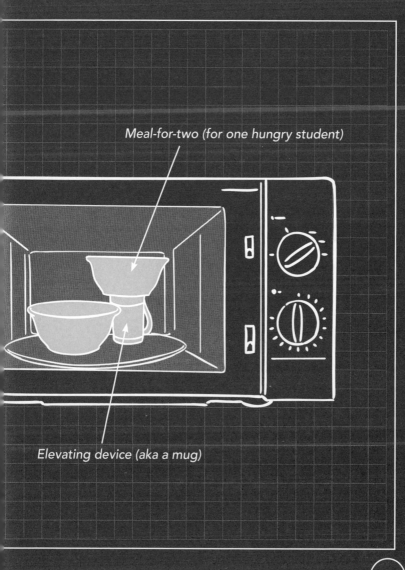

Meal-for-two (for one hungry student)

Elevating device (aka a mug)

TEXTBOOK GAME CHANGER

You're trying to read a textbook twice the size of you and the pages have a mind of their own. Keep them securely in place by clipping together the ones you've read with a binder clip. This should also act as a paperweight, leaving your hands free for all-important note-taking.

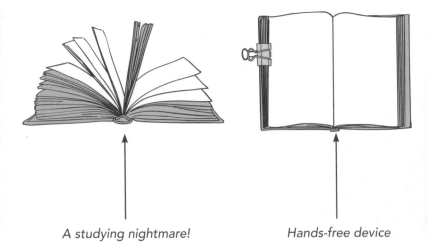

A studying nightmare!   *Hands-free device*

LAP TRAY

If you don't have a desk in your room to work at and you rest your laptop on your legs instead, use a lap tray with a cushion attached to put the laptop on. You will no longer have to endure the continual rush of hot air from the fan that leaves you sweating.

Save those thighs!

LAPTOP COOLER

Has your laptop ever overheated just sentences before you're about to finish an assignment? It's frustrating, especially if you didn't save your work (in which case you are just a fool). Prevent this from happening again by placing it on a couple of cardboard egg cartons. Sometimes all it needs is a little TLC.

Humble egg carton

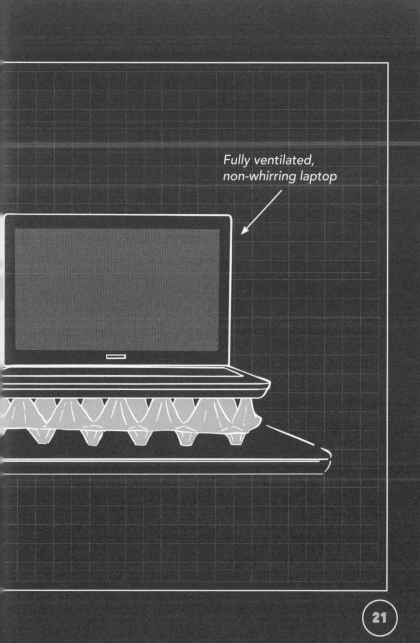

Fully ventilated, non-whirring laptop

DIY CORKSCREW

There's nothing worse when you're all set for pre-dinner drinks but you've bought a bottle of wine with a cork instead of a screw cap, and no one's got a corkscrew. Remove the fear of not being able to drink with your mates with this hack.

Find a trainer and put the bottom end of the bottle of wine in it. Find a sturdy wall and holding both bottle and shoe, securely bang the sole of the trainer against the wall. You should see the cork slowly move. Once it's in a grabbable position, pull the cork out of the bottle and pour a glass with a smug look on your face.

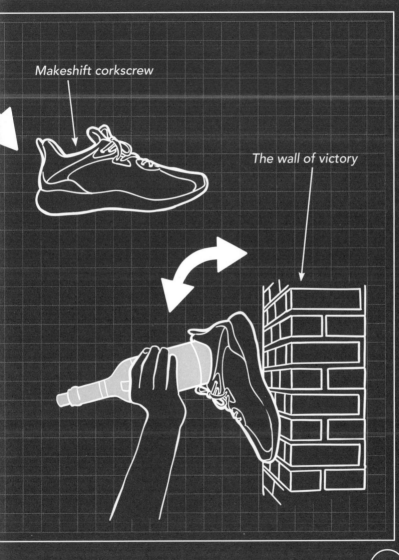

Makeshift corkscrew

The wall of victory

DIY CORKSCREW 2

If you don't have a corkscrew, a shoe or a wall, how on earth do you survive each day (see page 22)?! But no need to fear, as there's another hack for removing a cork from a wine bottle without a corkscrew (we've all been desperate at times!).

Grab a nail and hammer, and hammer the nail into the cork but not all the way in. Then, with the pronged end of the hammer, secure the nail and pull it away from the bottle. The cork should come out with the nail.

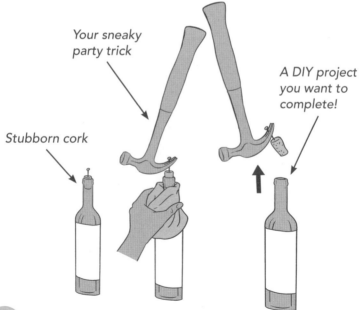

Your sneaky party trick

A DIY project you want to complete!

Stubborn cork

SHARPIE ERASERS

If you ever go on a student night out, especially if it's school fancy dress, don't be alarmed if you wake up the next day and find pen all over your body, furniture and walls. You might think you are doomed but with this hack you'll be able to erase all your Sharpie problems.

If it's on your clothes, hand sanitiser will remove it; for walls, use toothpaste or hairspray; on carpet, white vinegar; furniture, milk; ceramic or glass, one part baking soda and one part toothpaste.

The things we think we're good at when drunk

Luckily the landlord will never find out about this thanks to your secret stash of hairspray

INTERNET SIGNAL BOOSTER

The wifi in your room is rubbish but there's no way you're paying over the odds for super-duper spectacular speedy fibre-optic broadband (as quoted on numerous adverts). So, instead, why not use a drinks or food can to create a signal booster to increase speeds?

Wash the can thoroughly, leave it to dry, then remove the ring pull from the top. With a Stanley knife, pierce the can midway down and cut in a line up to the top, then down to the bottom. Then cut all the way round the bottom rim of the can to remove the base and around most of the top rim of the can, leaving one inch of it attached near the drinking hole. Add some sticky tack to the lid and secure it onto the router by inserting the antenna through the drinking hole.

Formerly a delicious fizzy drink

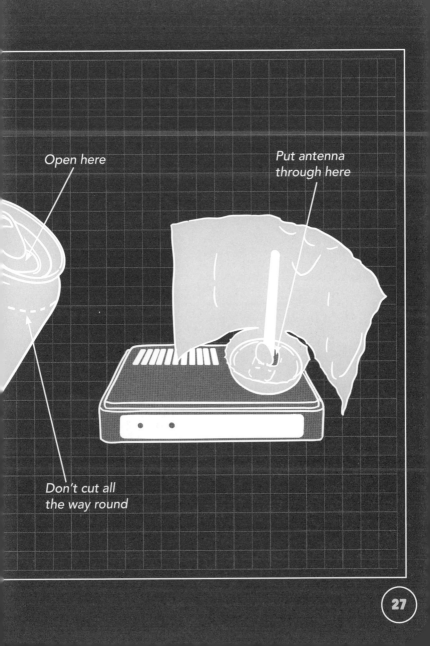

Open here

Put antenna
through here

Don't cut all
the way round

LECTURE HACKS

Is your note-taking too slow to keep up with what the lecturer is saying? Are you easily distracted by everything other than what you should be focusing on? This chapter's hacks will help you make the most out of your classroom time.

DISTRACTION PREVENTER

If you use a laptop in lectures, one of the positives is that you can search for anything related to the topic your lecturer is speaking about. One of the negatives is that the whole world is at your fingertips, including a lot of distracting websites. To make sure you're getting your money's worth (literally speaking if you're at university), you can download computer software to temporarily block the websites that send you into the depths of procrastination. Most products do cost a small amount of money, but it'll be well worth it when you pass with flying colours.

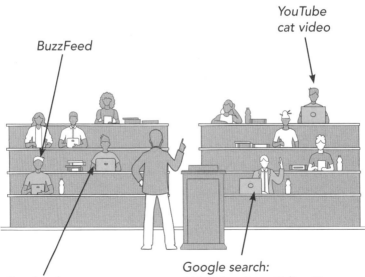

YouTube cat video

BuzzFeed

Facebook

Google search: 'What is existentialism?'

HANDOUTS ORGANISER

Although paper handouts seem to be a dying species, as most things are uploaded onto university portals, they are great for scribbling extra details in the margins and are worth keeping for revision. To benefit from them properly, and to keep them in an orderly fashion, try this hack.

Never stack your handouts in a pile, but buy a concertina file to put them in. Label each section of the file with the course module name. As soon as you get back from a lecture, place the handouts in the correct section of the file and facing the same way, so they are easy to see.

Handouts stored away (preferably not forever but until you need them)

Easy-to-read labels

WATCH A DOCUMENTARY

After your lecture, there's nothing better than tuning into some rubbish TV. However, as an alternative, why not find a documentary about the topic discussed in class that will help you to remember the information you learnt while also learning new things about it. You're still getting your dose of TV, just without the complicated love triangle.

Student relentlessly rewinding a documentary to make sure he doesn't miss out on any of the fascinating facts

LECTURE VOICE RECORDER

Buy a cheap voice recorder or download a phone app that allows you to record the length of your lectures and leave in a place that will pick up the speaker's voice. Using a recorder doesn't mean you shouldn't pay attention in class, but they are really helpful if you struggle to jot down relevant notes in the allotted time. Make sure you ask for permission from the university/professor first as some content could be copyrighted. (Don't worry about looking like an aspiring journo – it's quite a common lecture hack.)

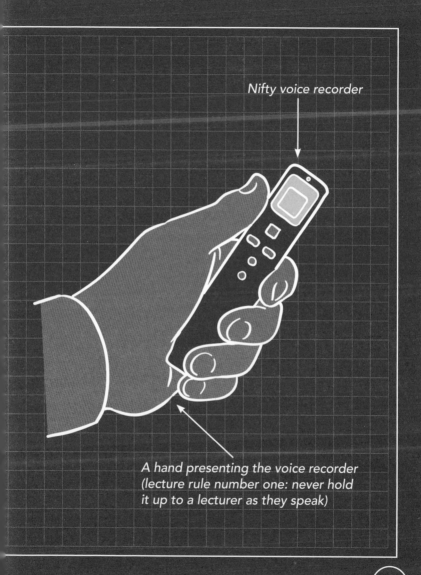

Nifty voice recorder

_A hand presenting the voice recorder
(lecture rule number one: never hold
it up to a lecturer as they speak)_

RESEARCH THE SUBJECT

Before your lecture you are usually given a brief overview on what it will be about. Instead of pushing this knowledge to the outer peripheries of your brain, be the intuitive student that you are and research the subject prior to the lecture. If you already know a little about the topic/person/book/theory, you'll be able to absorb the information your professor is excitedly relaying to you a lot better.

They have no idea what's going on

You, feeling smug with the power of knowledge

CUSHION COMFORTER

When you've got back-to-back lectures, don't make yourself suffer any more than you have to by sitting on a wooden bench for the entire day. Instead, take a cushion with you to create a more comfortable environment in which to learn. If you don't want to lug a cumbersome cushion around with you on campus all day, buy an inflatable one that fits easily into your bag.

Extortionate tuition fees and we don't even get a complimentary cushion

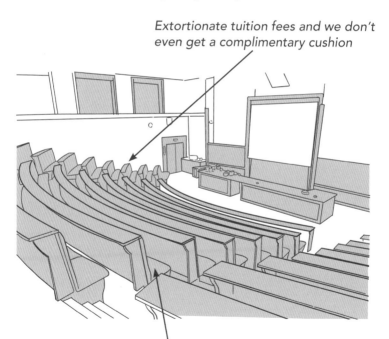

An aerial view of the most abominable lecture seats known to students

NOTES ON NOTE-TAKING

Take a look around you in a lecture and you will find a huge amount of your peers frantically scribbling every word your lecturer says into their notepads. Don't be like these people; you are smarter than them. Use abbreviations instead – such as the following ones you are now going to quickly learn before your next lecture:

approx.	approximately
b/c	because
b/4	before
c.	approximately, roughly, about (abbreviation for the Latin 'circa')
cf.	compared to, in comparison with
cp.	compare
def.	definition

diff.	different, difference
ea.	each
fr.	from
gen.	general
impt.	important
NB	important, notice this, note well
nec.	necessary
pt.	point
re.	regarding, about
sim.	similar
s/t	something
T.	theory, theoretical
w/	with
w/o	without
v.	very
viz.	namely, that is to say
vs.	against
≠	does not equal, is not the same as, does not result in
↑	increase, rise, growth
↓	decrease, fall, shrinkage
∴	therefore, thus
→	leads on to, produces, causes
/	per (e.g. £50/day instead of '50 pounds per day')

HOUSEHOLD HACKS

Do you have to awkwardly prop up your tablet or hold it in your hand to watch TV? Do you wish you could create more space to fit your food on the two fridge shelves you have been given? Are you constantly having to buy new phone chargers as your housemates accidentally take yours? This chapter offers all the solutions to your student-house problems.

FRAME IT

Ever heard of Washi tape? I hadn't until I went to university. Spruce up your walls by 'framing' your photographs and postcards using this low-tack masking tape that shouldn't make any marks on the walls, unlike its counterpart, sticky tack. There is a variety of patterned, glittery and foil tapes on the high street to choose from, so when you get bored of a frame you can switch it without spending a fortune!

Just like the National Gallery

MAKESHIFT TV MOUNT

It's difficult to justify buying a TV when you have a tablet that you can do more on (and that goes for everybody, not just students). But when your arm becomes achy from holding it and your neck hurts from looking down to see it, maybe you should try this hack.

Buy some adhesive hooks and secure them to your wall (only if you have permission to do so from your landlord) so that your tablet will fit nicely perched on top. Put on a good series, get comfy and do a little jazz-hand dance to experience the freedom of going hands-free.

Just like a 50-inch plasma-screen TV

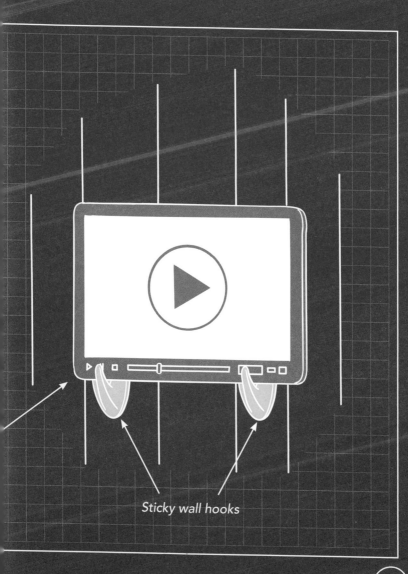

Sticky wall hooks

NOOK-AND-CRANNY HOOVER EXTENSION

Is your laptop keyboard or phone speaker really grubby? Are places you can't get to building up with dirt? Find a lid that has a pointy tip (DIY hair-dye bottles or squeezy sauce-bottle lids usually do) and attach it with sticky tack to your vacuum-cleaner pipe. Get vacuuming and clear out the year-old crumbs in a flash!

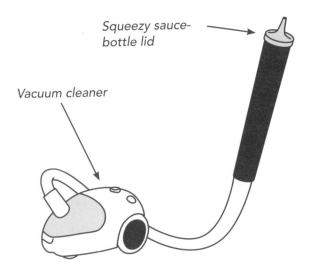

Squeezy sauce-bottle lid

Vacuum cleaner

FANBREEZE

Is your dirty washing building up so much that it's giving off disturbing smells? Keep your room constantly clean, or at least disguise the pong, by taping dryer sheets to a fan. The air generated from it will smell like a field of fresh flowers.

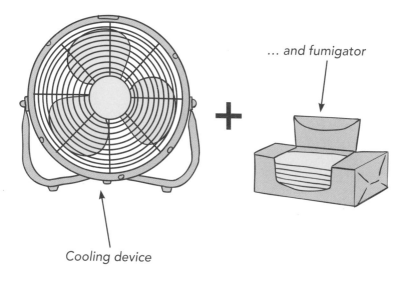

... and fumigator

Cooling device

BAR-STOOL BIN

Are you planning a party and there aren't enough bins for all the litter that's bound to be created? If this is the case, turn your bar stool into a bin by putting it upside down and placing a bag in it. You may not have a seat to sit on but at least your room won't be messy!

Bin bag

Turned-over stool-cum-rubbish-bin (don't turn the stool over to sit on when it's acting as a bin)

BOTTLE STACKER

Fridge space comes at a premium when you share a kitchen with other people, and finding ways to maximise your designated food and drink area is a never-ending task.

However, this hack should help you in your trials. Before you put your bottles/cans in the fridge, attach a binder clip onto one of the rungs on your shelf. This acts as a buffer to stop those pesky bottles rolling away, and means you can now stack them in a neat and orderly fashion.

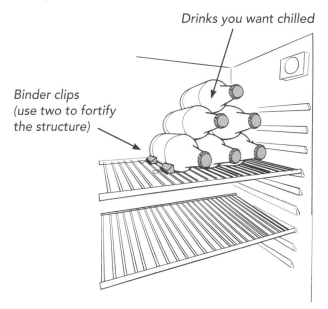

Drinks you want chilled

Binder clips
(use two to fortify
the structure)

AIRTIGHT SPAGHETTI CONTAINER

Instead of keeping spaghetti in the plastic it comes in, where the strands can easily spill everywhere and become stale, use a clean and empty Pringles can to store them. It will also save a lot of space in your storage cupboards where space is at a premium – though it might give any crisp-stealing housemates a surprise when they raid your cupboard late at night!

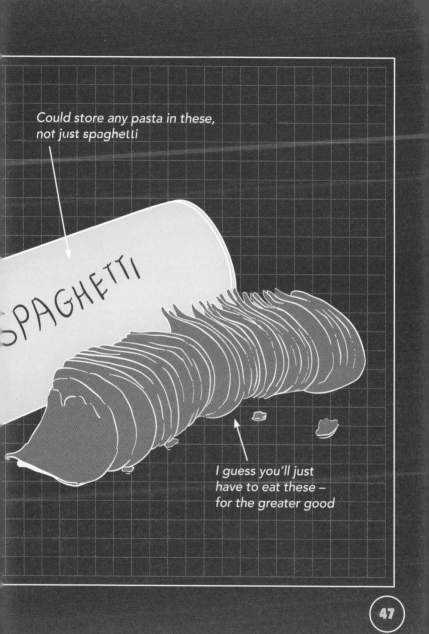

DE-CREASER

Do you have a fancy night out or official ceremony to go to but have just realised all your clothes are wrinkled? Try this quick fix.

Take the aforementioned clothes and put them in a tumble dryer with a clean but damp tea towel for 5 minutes. They should come out smooth and silky, ready for you to look like a boss.

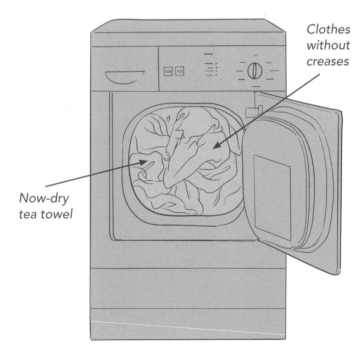

Clothes without creases

Now-dry tea towel

RED WINE STAIN REMOVER

Red wine is great when you're drinking it but bad when you spill it on the carpet of a property that isn't yours. If this happens, don't make matters worse by spreading the stain with a wet cloth. Instead, pour salt over the stain when it's still wet. Leave overnight (carry on drinking if you must) then hoover up the salt particles in the morning. The stain should be gone, or at least very faint.

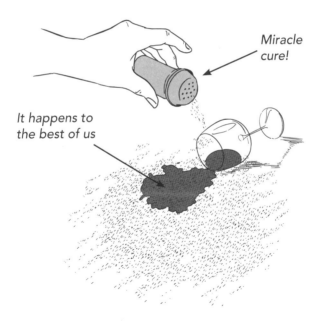

Miracle cure!

It happens to the best of us

NO-HASSLE CLEAN FRIDGE

Never wash a fridge shelf again with this hack. Take the shelves out, wrap cling film around them and put them back in place. After a few months, when they're looking a bit dirty, simply remove the cling film from the shelves and replace with a fresh lot.

Shelf wrapper

No need to worry about dreaded apple shelf stains any longer!

TOOTHBRUSH SEPARATOR

Do you ever get weirded out by people sharing toothbrushes or even toothbrushes touching? It's fine to have some hygiene principles as a student, you know! Avoid your housemates' toothbrushes having a rendezvous with yours with this nifty DIY device.

Place elastic bands around a glass to form a grid shape and slot the toothbrushes into the spaces in the grid: your toothbrush will be safe for the rest of term.

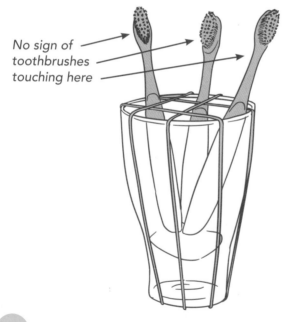

No sign of toothbrushes touching here

KITCHEN SURFACE EXTENDER

Do you find that there's no space to prepare meals in your kitchen? Are you tired of jostling for space while three other people are trying to cook their pasta? Open one of your kitchen drawers and place your chopping board over the top when you want to slice and dice your ingredients.

Yes, of course students eat vegetables

Drawer posing as surface extender

POST HOLDER

Never forget where you put your letters with this hack. Cut a slit in a tennis ball and attach the back of it to a wall by placing Velcro on both and sticking them together (check with your landlord for permission first). Whenever you receive post put it in its mouth so you remember to open it later.

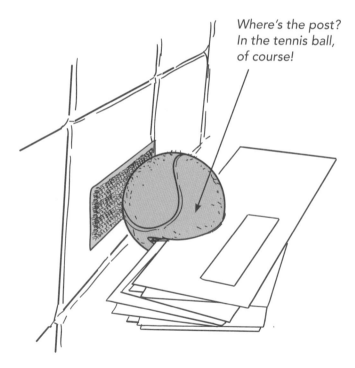

Where's the post? In the tennis ball, of course!

PHONE-CHARGER IDENTIFIER

House-sharing can bring about several issues, one of which is not knowing whose charger is whose. To avoid mixing yours up with your housemates', wrap your charger plug with some decorative Washi tape (perhaps you have some left over from your photo-wall-decorating spree – see page 39) – problem solved. Now you just have to argue over whose decorating skills are the most on point.

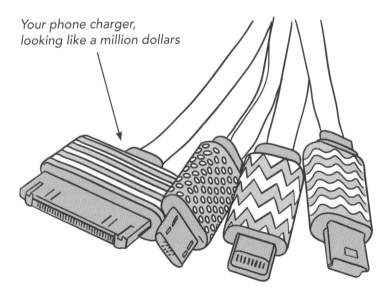

Your phone charger, looking like a million dollars

TIDY-UP AND STORAGE HACKS

Does your stationery not have a home? Do you have too much to do but are never sure what you should do first? In this chapter you will learn all the tips and tricks to help you become the most organised student of them all.

TOILET-ROLL ORGANISERS

Change your perception of the futility of empty toilet rolls with this hack. Whenever you get to the end of your toilet roll, save the cardboard to make them into stationery holders – your desk will thank you for it. Just cover the bottom (to protect the desk from getting pen marks on it), and then put a weight in it so that the tube doesn't fall over when it's used. To disguise them, wrap coloured tissue paper or wrapping paper around them. Instead of paying out for tatty plastic holders, you're creating a clutter-free desk without spending a penny (ho, ho).

Toilet-paper tubes wrapped in pretty paper (honest!)

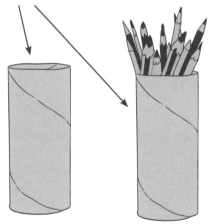

No sign of clutter on desk

Other uses for empty toilet rolls are:

Keeping leads and wires tangle-free, tidy and labelled.

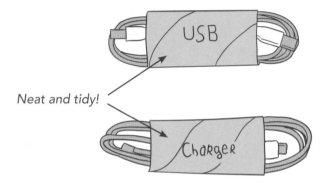

USB

Neat and tidy!

Charger

Store gift wrap without it unravelling by cutting a slit lengthways up the toilet roll and wrapping it around the paper.

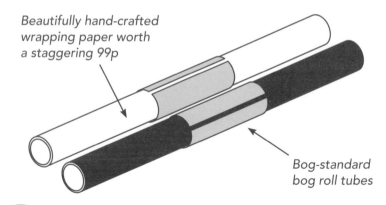

Beautifully hand-crafted wrapping paper worth a staggering 99p

Bog-standard bog roll tubes

And you can even use them to create gift boxes:

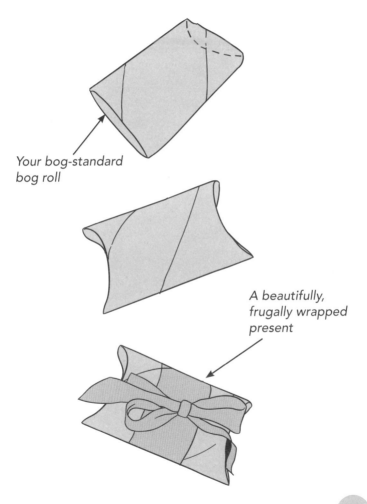

Your bog-standard bog roll

A beautifully, frugally wrapped present

WARDROBE SPACE SAVER

You've moved out of your parents' house with all your clothes that fitted snugly into your spacious double wardrobe, and you've arrived at your student accommodation to find you only have a small cubby hole as a makeshift wardrobe. That is where this hack comes in handy.

Save the ring pulls from cans of soft drinks and beer and thread them onto the hook of a hanger, letting them rest at the bottom where the hook meets the hanger. You have now created a loop to attach another hanger, thus doubling the capacity.

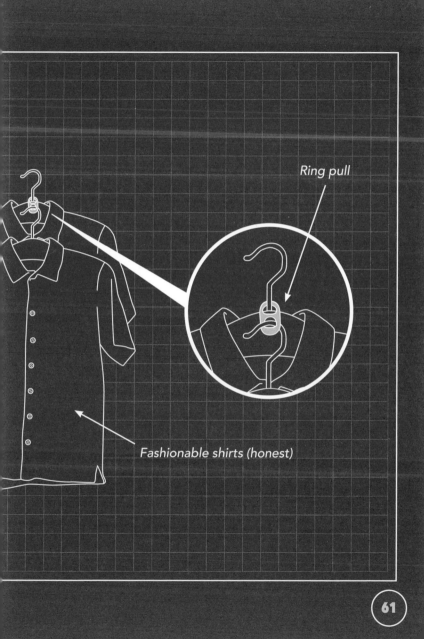

Ring pull

Fashionable shirts (honest)

WARDROBE SPACE SAVER 2

If you struggle for wardrobe space and you don't have enough hangers to accommodate all your clothes, try this alternative hack. Using either a coat-hanger or the wardrobe rail, attach shower hooks (available at most DIY stores) onto them and then hang your clothes on by the belt loops of your trousers, skirts and shorts or the tag you sometimes find at the top of shirts, T-shirts and jumpers. You can even store belts, attaching them with the belt clasps, and scarfs on them.

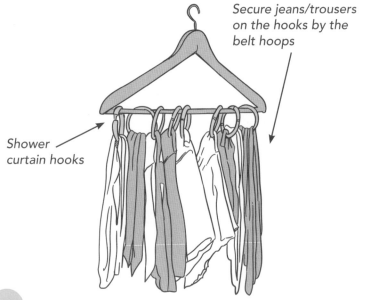

Secure jeans/trousers on the hooks by the belt hoops

Shower curtain hooks

DRAWER SPACE MAXIMISER

Become a clothes-folding expert with this hack and save ample cupboard space. First you need to know how to fold your T-shirts into small, neat squares. Then you need to stack the small T-shirt squares one on top of the other. Place the pile in your drawer sideways on so you can see all your T-shirts at a glance. You have increased the capacity of your drawers and at the same time made it easier to extract the top you want to wear.

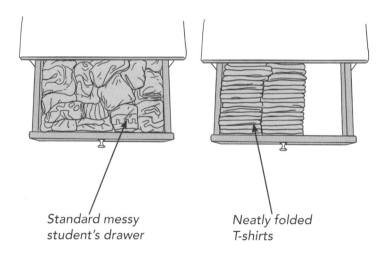

Standard messy
student's drawer

Neatly folded
T-shirts

STATIONERY STORAGE

Over the years, have you built up a huge collection of pens, notebooks and other school supplies, and don't know where to keep them? Repurpose a plastic shoe organiser to help store your stationery in an orderly fashion. Label each section so that the items are easy to find and you know where to put them back again once you've finished using them.

Pens, etc. bulging out of their compartments

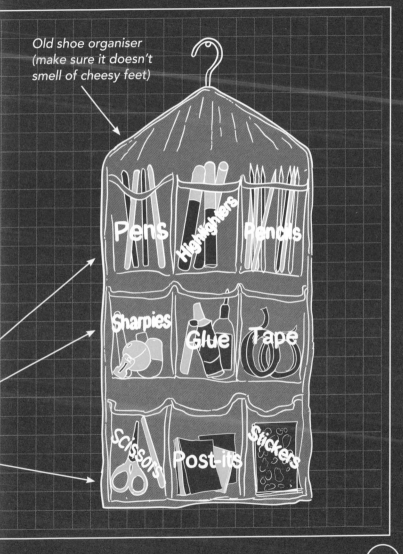

Old shoe organiser (make sure it doesn't smell of cheesy feet)

Pens

Highlighters

Pencils

Sharpies

Glue

Tape

Scissors

Post-its

Stickers

SEASONAL CLOTHING STORAGE

If you are struggling for wardrobe space, yet half your clothes are for the summer and it's blooming freezing outside, pack them in a suitcase and keep them tucked away until it starts to get warmer. Then switch the clothes around and you've doubled your wardrobe space. Genius!

Maybe try to pack them a bit neater than this...

It may feel like you're going on holiday, but unfortunately you're not

CREATE MORE KITCHEN CUPBOARDS

We're always looking for extra space in our cupboards, especially when you've only been allotted one measly cupboard in your shared kitchen, but why not think outside the box? Literally.

Use the space on top of your cupboards to store items that aren't required daily but are still handy to have in plastic containers and wire racks. This will make it easier to get things down when you need them without creating a kitchen avalanche.

Things above the kitchen cupboards

Things in the kitchen cupboards

TOILETRIES HOLDER

Toiletries take up a lot of space and can be awkward to get to without them all falling over when they are standing up in a row. Use a wine rack to store them horizontally and in a neat and tidy group.

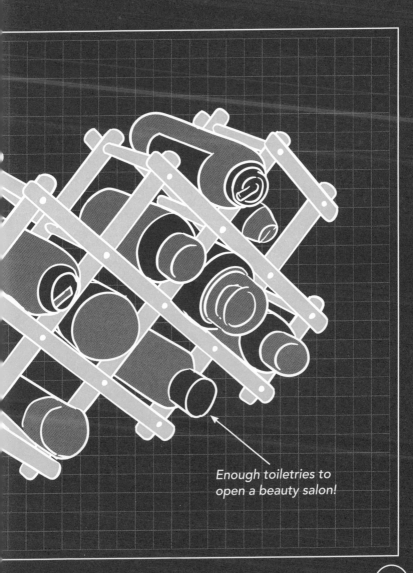

Enough toiletries to open a beauty salon!

CLEANING-PRODUCT HANGER

We usually store our cleaning products (or let them build up) under the sink. To increase the cupboard space under your sink, hang the bottles onto the sink's pipe by the handles. Then you have room on the bottom to keep your cloths, sponges etc.

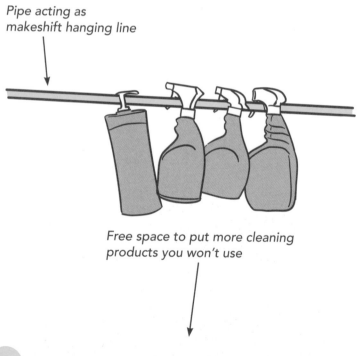

Pipe acting as makeshift hanging line

Free space to put more cleaning products you won't use

FILING AWAY KITCHEN PRODUCTS

Does it take double the time to cook a meal because you are endlessly searching for things you need but can't find? Make your household kitchen products easy to get to by storing them in a file organiser/magazine holder. Put the smaller items at the front and the taller items at the back so they are easier to see.

Does this mean your files are now sprawled all over your floor?!

BED LINEN SPACE SAVER

If you have spare linen sets and they take up a lot of space in your bedroom, use this hack to make them more compact. Fold the bedsheet, duvet cover and pillowcases as you usually would, but leave one pillowcase spare. Take the folded sheets and slide them into the unfolded pillowcase.

Looks good enough to sleep in —

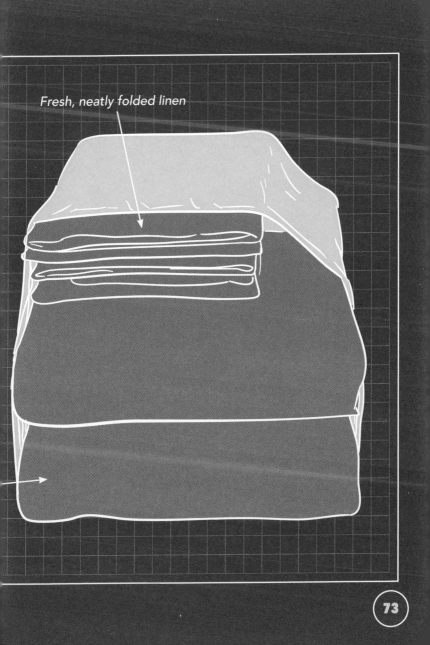

Fresh, neatly folded linen

BREAD-TAG LABELS

Have you ever spent a silly amount of time trying to work out which plug is connected to which electrical item? Never mix them up again with this hack.

Save some bread tags (different-coloured ones if you can) and label each with the name of one of your appliances (e.g. phone charger, hair dryer, kettle, microwave) with a marker pen. Then place the bread tag on its respective cable and you have your own nifty labelling system.

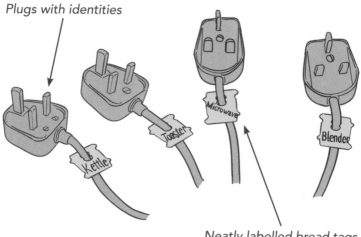

Plugs with identities

Neatly labelled bread tags

KITCHEN-ROLL HOLDER

If you can't afford a fancy kitchen-roll dispenser, take a plastic clothes hanger and remove most of the bottom section of it with a saw (be careful not to chop any fingers off in the process), so it can hold a standard kitchen roll (you should be able to flex it to fit it on, and then let it ping back into shape to hold onto the roll). Attach it to a cupboard handle and *voilà*, you have a cheap and cheerful paper-roll holder.

Grab-and-go device for when you spill your Bolognese on the carpet

CORD TIDY

Be the neat freak you've always wanted to be with this hack to prevent your wires from tangling up into a messy ball. Grab some binder clips and attach them to the edge of a table. Then arrange your loose wires (e.g. charger cables) by threading each through a separate clip and letting them hang there neatly until you need them.

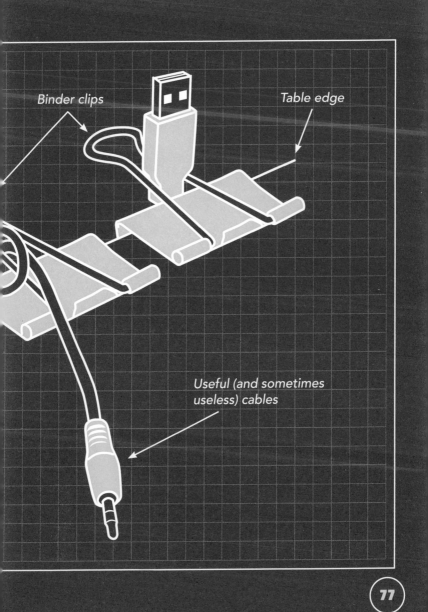

Binder clips

Table edge

Useful (and sometimes useless) cables

STUDY
AND EXAM
HACKS

Do you worry about your sleeping patterns during exam periods? Do your nerves get the better of you? The hacks in this chapter will help you to prepare, live and feel better when the exam- and assignment-seasons start.

WORD FINDER

If you're struggling to remember a word that you know would sound impressive in your essay, use the website wordhippo.com. As long as you know one of the word's synonyms or antonyms, a word that it rhymes with or what the meaning of the word is, more often than not the site will come up with the word you're looking for. Now you can breeze through assignments without being stuck for hours mid-sentence, then forgetting what the sentence was you wanted to write.

A Shakespeare in the making!

LOUD AND PROUD

No, this hack isn't about passing wind audaciously. However, it does require using another orifice. Whenever you need to remember facts or figures for an exam, try saying the words aloud, as they're 50 per cent more likely to sink in. It's also a great method to use when you are reading through an assignment before handing it in to make sure there aren't any awkwardly phrased sentences in it.

MAXIMISE BRAIN POWER

It might seem like the silliest thing to do before an exam, but it has been proven that around 20 minutes of exercise before you sit a test can help to improve brain activity, as it stimulates memory.

You aren't required to run a PB marathon but, if you usually drive or use public transport, a fast-paced walk to the exam building from where you live could be really beneficial. Just make sure that doing the extra mile won't make you late – you don't want to waste all that extra cleverness by missing your exam!

A super-charged brain ——————

BECOME A TEACHER

If you've been trying to get your head around a theory and you think you're almost there, test your knowledge by teaching someone else. It helps if they know the subject; a classmate would be the perfect pupil as they can let you know if you're going wrong. Or, if the classmate hasn't spent time studying the topic, you might be saving them from failing the course in the process!

*All your wonderful knowledge
(I'm sure it's here somewhere)*

Teacher-you

BECOME A
SEARCH-BAR BOSS

Most of the time, we prepare for taking an exam or writing an assignment by researching everything surrounding the topic. Much of this will be done via books, periodicals, journals and the internet. Although we can't change how long a specific book takes to find in the library, we can help reduce the stress of trying to find something on the web with this guide to search-engine hacks:

- **DASHES** - use these when you want to exclude a word from the search, e.g. titanic -movie. This is helpful when a word has lots of different meanings.

RELATED - use this to search for websites similar to one you already know, e.g. related:psychologytoday.com

SITE - use this when you only want results from a specific domain, e.g. healthy living site:bbc.co.uk

~ **TILDES** - use a tilde (~) when you want to search a word and its synonyms, e.g. tennis ~lesson.

•• **TWO FULL POINTS** - use these (..) between numbers when you want to search for anything in that range, e.g. American literature 1800..1850.

"" **QUOTATION MARKS** - inserting your search term in double quotation marks, e.g. "I think, therefore I am", tells the search engine to only look for that specific phrase.

GIVE YOUR WORK A FONT BOOST

Using fancy fonts for assignments is always a no-no, but have you wondered which font is the easiest to read? According to a number of studies, serif fonts are better for print and sans-serif fonts are easier to read on screen. If you aren't a typeface aficionado, serif fonts have little flicks on the ends of the letters while sans-serif fonts are typically rounder and cleaner. Next time you're typing up your notes or draft essays to print off and read through, it might be worth considering which font to use a little more than you usually would to make things as easy for yourself as possible.

This is easy to read ← *Good for printed work*

This is easy to read ← *Good for on-screen work*

This is not easy to read ← *Good luck passing*

This is not easy to read ← *It's a fail*

TAKE BREAKS

You may feel the only option to pass a course is to cram in as much revision as possible in a day, but - ironically thanks to studies - science tells us that this isn't conducive to retaining information. Instead, it is best to revise little and often, which does mean you have to start the revision earlier than you'd like to but gives you an excuse to go to that game of Ultimate Frisbee after all.

You and your friends, hard at work

All the work you'll do much better after just one more game...

SLEEP-CYCLE PLANNER

If you have an early morning exam and are worried you'll still feel tired during it, try this hack.

Because your brain sleeps in 90-minute cycles, time your sleep with these cycles to help you avoid waking up right in the deep sleep stage. Work out what time you need to be up the next morning and count backwards in blocks of 90 minutes until you reach the time you think it's likely you'll be able to fall asleep. For example, if you need to be up at 7 a.m., try going to sleep at either 10 or 11.30 p.m.

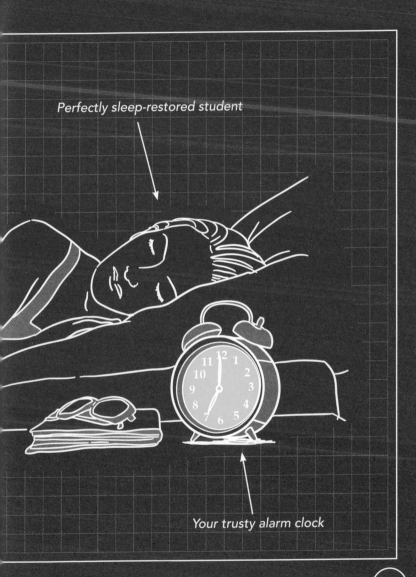

Perfectly sleep-restored student

Your trusty alarm clock

PROBLEM EXTRACTOR

In the run-up to exams, it is usually more difficult to go to sleep at night because there are a million and one things flying round your head that you need to remember. Whenever you do have exams or assignments looming, place a notepad and pen close to your bed so that whenever you think of something, you can quickly transfer it to paper and put your mind at ease.

The Diaries of A. N. Other
(it could become a bestseller
at some point, you never know)

CHEWING-GUM GAME CHANGER

Regardless of what your teachers used to say about chewing gum in the school classroom, studies suggest that it can help you to concentrate while you are revising. The science behind it is that breathing while chewing gum allows more oxygen to pass through the lungs than when breathing normally, and this can increase levels of alertness.

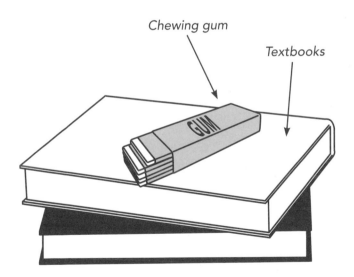

Chewing gum

Textbooks

STUDENTS DON'T CRY

When the stress of exams piles up on you and the last straw is the takeaway that was meant to be delivered 30 minutes ago still hasn't arrived, try forcing a laugh instead of crying. It helps to relieve all the pent-up tension, and will make you feel a lot better. Make sure your favourite funny YouTube video is easily accessible for those overwhelming moments that can push you over the edge.

The release of stress is palpable

ANXIETY-LIFTING LAVENDER

Lavender is claimed to decrease your heart rate, and rubbing it on your temples has a calming effect. Create your own lavender essential oil with this hack.

Pick off the lavender flowers and leaves from their stems and leave to dry in the shade or wrap in a cloth - this process could take up to a week. Gently crush the lavender, either with the back of a spoon or your fingers, and place in a small jar. Add almond oil to the jar until it covers the lavender and leave to soak for at least 48 hours, but longer if possible. Then dab a finger's worth onto your temples and chill out.

Freshly crushed lavender

Let the oil meet the lavender

PLASTIC-SLEEVE WHITEBOARD

Use a plastic sleeve for your workings-out. Scribble on it with a dry-erase pen and it can become your very own makeshift whiteboard. Not only is it great for quick calculations in lessons, you can also use it when you are working out your monthly budget. Once you don't need the information anymore, use a tissue to wipe it off – it's almost as good as an Etch-a-Sketch (not quite though).

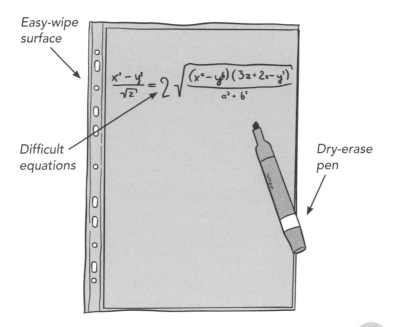

Easy-wipe surface

Difficult equations

$$\frac{x^3 - y^2}{\sqrt{2}} = 2\sqrt{\frac{(x^a - y^6)(3z + 2x - y^3)}{a^3 + b^2}}$$

Dry-erase pen

HIGHLIGHTER HELPER

When you're revising, make important words spring off the page by using different colour highlighter pens for different themes or subjects. Use sticky labels to remind you which colour corresponds to which theme and get highlighter happy.

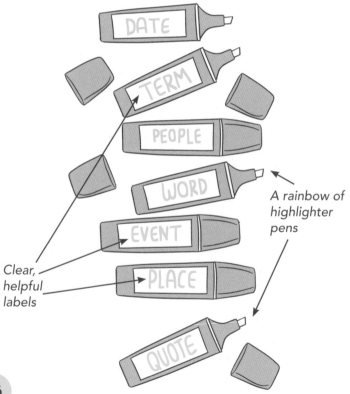

A rainbow of highlighter pens

Clear, helpful labels

TEXTBOOK COLOUR CODING

With a selection of different-coloured highlighters, colour code the page edges of your textbooks for each different module you have that term/semester. When you wake up with 5 minutes to spare before your lesson starts, you can quickly grab your books without having to worry if you picked up the correct ones.

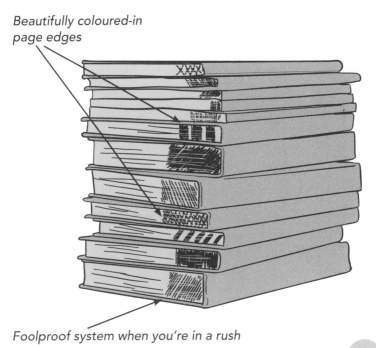

Beautifully coloured-in page edges

Foolproof system when you're in a rush

HEALTH AND WELL-BEING HACKS

Do you want to do more exercise but can't afford a gym membership? Do you always forget to drink water throughout the day and end up giving yourself a headache when it's time to write an assignment? In this chapter you will find essential health and well-being hacks to make you feel like a better, fresher you, especially as you'll be partying a lot more than you are used to!

HYDRATION REMINDER

Unless you live somewhere really hot, the recommended water intake for adults is 1.2 litres a day. Remind yourself to drink the correct amount of water with this hack.

To help you remember, mark the hours of the day on a 1-litre water bottle with permanent marker at 200 ml intervals, starting at 8 a.m. You'll finish your bottle by noon so then you can refill it for the afternoon. By 6 p.m. you will have consumed eight glasses of water and will have probably taken one extra trip to the toilet than you're used to.

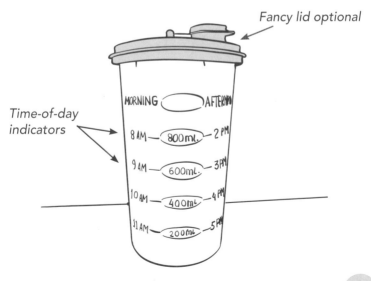

Fancy lid optional

Time-of-day indicators

MORNING   AFTERNOON

8 AM — 800mL — 2 PM

9 AM — 600mL — 3 PM

10 AM — 400mL — 4 PM

11 AM — 200mL — 5 PM

EASY-TO-CLEAN BLENDER

You want to be healthy and start having fruit smoothies, but cleaning the blender each time you have one is putting you off. With this hack, you'll be making unlimited amounts.

Once you've used the blender, fill it a quarter-full with water and a squirt of washing-up liquid. Then turn the blender on and let it whirl for a few seconds. Lastly, give it a rinse and it'll be squeaky clean and ready to use again.

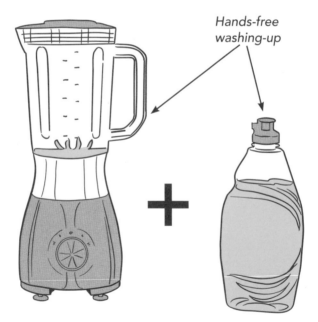

Hands-free washing-up

RAINY-DAY MUSIC DEVICE PROTECTOR

The rain can't stop you from going for a run but it could ruin the device from which you play music. And without music, you can't run. Make your device waterproof by wrapping cling film around it and run whenever you fancy, all year round. You can even change your music with the cling film wrapped around your phone – perfect!

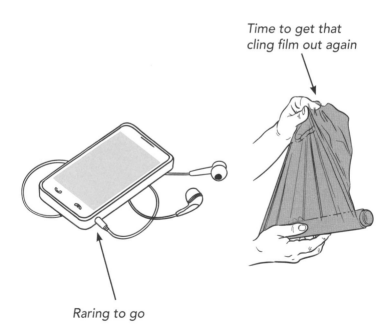

Time to get that cling film out again

Raring to go

CHILLED-WATER MAKER

Ever want ice-cold water during exercise but don't want to have to wait until your bottle of water in the freezer defrosts? Next time, fill your water bottle half full and place it in the freezer on its side. Just before you go out, remove the bottle from the freezer and fill the other half with cold water. The ice will make the water really cold and the water will make the ice melt, leaving you with water that stays perfectly chilled for a long time.

Empty freezer compartment (if only!)

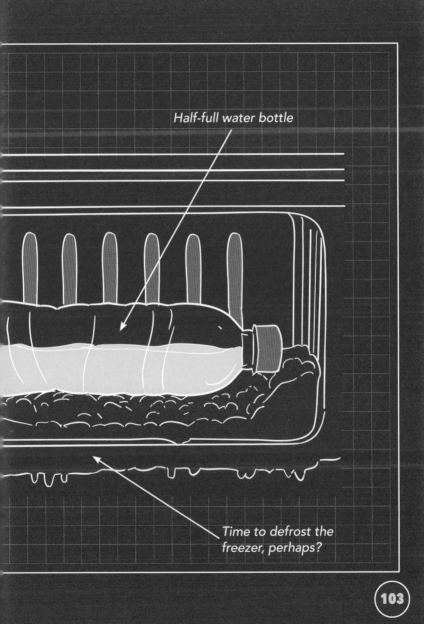

Half-full water bottle

Time to defrost the freezer, perhaps?

POSTURE FIXER

When you have seven assignments due in at the same time, you'll find yourself sitting at your computer for hours. It's easy to get into bad posture habits and there's nothing worse than suffering from bad backache when you have no alternative but to sit down and complete an essay. To help you sit up straight, roll up a towel and place it between the chair and your lower back (where your natural arch is). It'll feel uncomfortable at first but will be a back saver (not breaker) in the long run.

An enviable posture

Secret weapon

USE SMALLER PLATES AND BOWLS

The average size of plates and bowls is much bigger than it used to be, which can only mean that our portion sizes are growing. Be mindful of how much you eat by buying the smallest plates and bowls you can find and avoid piling them high with extra food - the point is to reduce your portion sizes to a healthy amount. You'll be surprised by how little you need to feel full.

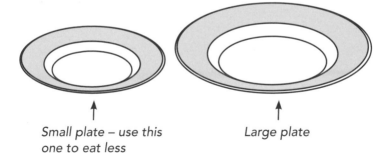

↑
Small plate – use this one to eat less

↑
Large plate

PLATE PLANNER

Personalise your small plate (see p.105) with portion guidelines to make sure you are getting the recommended amount of nutrients. With a Sharpie, divide your plate into three sections. Draw a horizontal line across the middle of the plate, then draw another line vertically at the halfway point of one of the two semicircles. Label the biggest portion 'fruits and vegetables' and label the other two equally sized portions 'protein' and 'starch'. Make it look as aesthetically pleasing as possible. To set the design, place the plate in the oven at 175°C for about 30 minutes. Never feel like you've accidentally over-indulged again.

A functional, but not necessarily beautiful, personalised plate

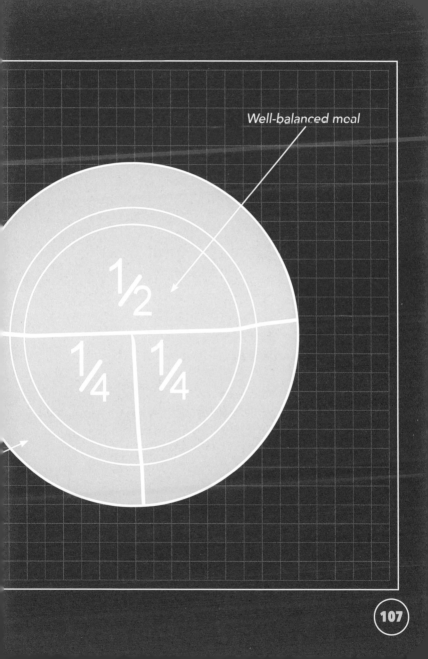

Well-balanced meal

1/2

1/4 1/4

NON-DRIP ICE PACKS

You've woken up after a night of partying to find that you've pulled a muscle or a part of your body is swollen. The first thing you do is grab a bag of frozen peas or ice cubes to help reduce the pain/swelling. However, it doesn't take long before you are left with something that's slightly warm and dripping wet. To prevent this, use non-drip ice packs instead. Soak a sponge in water and seal it in a reusable sandwich bag, then place it in the freezer. (Prepare a few at once if you're prone to suffering from injuries or swelling.) When you need to, apply the sponge in the bag to the affected area without worrying about soaking everything in your vicinity.

Zip-lock bag

Melted ice

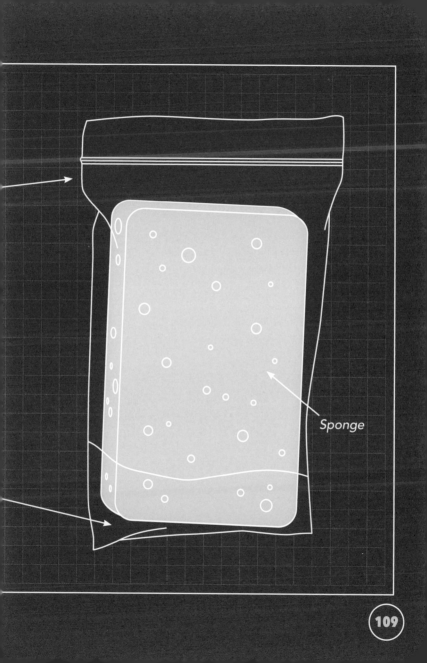

Sponge

DIY AFTERSUN

A super-effective way of treating sunburn (must be too much outdoor revision) and super-cheap too! In a large mug, brew three regular tea bags. Let the tea cool down, adding ice cubes to help speed up the process. Wait until the water is completely cold, as hot water exacerbates skin burn. Soak a flannel in this cold solution and dab onto the affected area. Let the tea soak into the skin, then reapply a few more times. Leave for a couple of hours or overnight and notice the results when you wash it off.

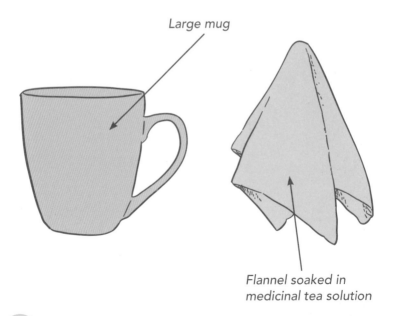

Large mug

Flannel soaked in medicinal tea solution

20/20/20

When you sit at your computer for most of the day and the glare of the screen gets too much, sometimes you find yourself glaring back without the ability to put together a sentence. Reduce eye strain and soreness by making sure that every 20 minutes looking at your screen is followed by at least 20 seconds of looking at something that is 20 feet away (exact measurements aren't necessary as long as the spot is in the distance).

An essential part of your work routine

DIY GYM

Don't pay crazy amounts of money on going to a gym when you can create your own at home with these hacks:

DIY GYM:
TOWEL WARM-UP

Warm up your upper body by rotating your arms in circle-like movements holding a towel.

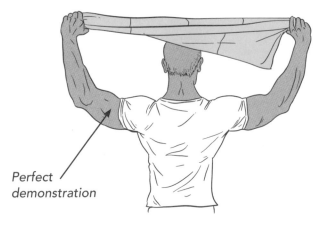

Perfect demonstration

Warm up your arms by holding a towel with both hands behind your back and slowly moving it up and down.

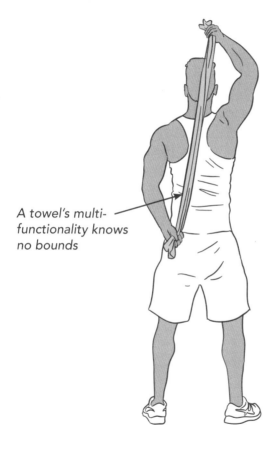

A towel's multi-functionality knows no bounds

DIY GYM: DUMB-BELLS

Use canned food or bottled water instead of dumb-bells. Holding one can/bottle in each hand, lift both arms so they are parallel with your shoulders. Hold for 10 seconds, then lower your arms slowly. Do three reps of ten with 2 minutes' rest in between each rep.

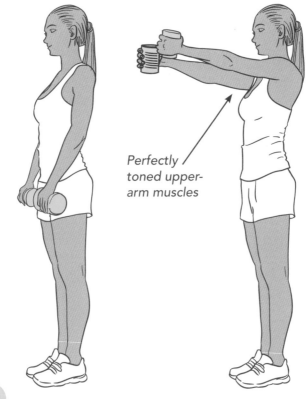

Perfectly toned upper-arm muscles

DIY GYM: STEPPER

Use stairs for cardio workouts or jump squats. Run down them and jump up them, for instance, or see how many times you can go up and down them within a certain time-frame.

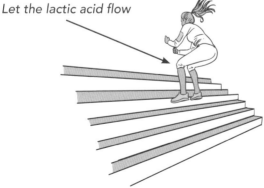

Let the lactic acid flow

DIY GYM: STRENGTHENING EXERCISES USING A SOFA

Stretch out your body lengthways, facing away from the sofa, and hold yourself up by placing your hands facing forwards on the sofa. Lower your bum so it's almost touching the floor and lift up until you reach your stretched-out position. Do three reps of ten with 2 minutes' rest in between each rep.

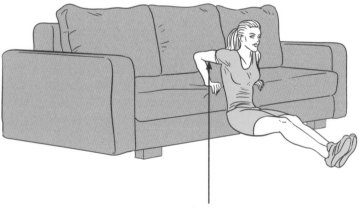

Feel the burn!

DIY GYM: STRENGTHENING EXERCISES USING A SOFA 2

Sit on a sofa without supporting your back, then lift your legs straight out in front of you off the floor and rotate them slowly in a clockwise movement. Do three reps of ten with 2 minutes' rest in between each rep.

Do this while watching TV and you're golden

DIY GYM: SOFA OR WALL LUNGES

You can use a sofa to perform half squats by standing with your back towards it. Lower yourself as if you were about to sit and hover in that position, making sure your back is vertical, for 10 seconds. Then gradually straighten yourself to standing position. If you don't have a sofa, support your back against a wall and lower yourself until in a sitting position. Do three reps of twenty with 2 minutes' rest in between each rep.

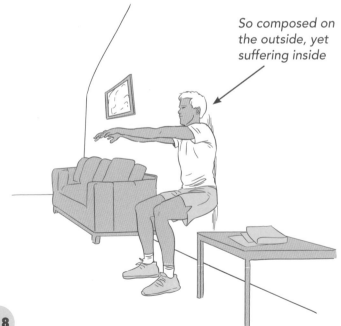

So composed on the outside, yet suffering inside

DIY GYM: PILLOW POWER EXERCISES

Hold a pillow just below shoulder height with your arms stretched out and jump from one foot to the other lifting your knees high enough so they hit the pillow. Do five reps of ten with 2 minutes' rest in between each rep.

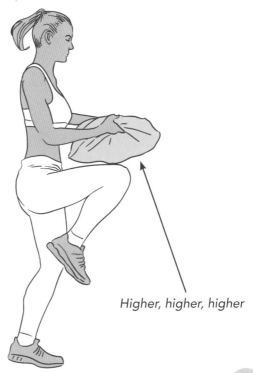

Higher, higher, higher

DIY GYM: PILLOW POWER EXERCISES 2

Use both hands to hold the edges of a pillow and swing it back and forth as if swinging a tennis racket - use a wall to stop the swing, making sure you don't accidently punch the wall with your hand. Do five reps of twenty with 2 minutes' rest in between each rep.

What a great stress-reliever

DIY GYM: TENNIS-BALL CORE EXERCISES

Prepare yourself in plank position and put a tennis ball on the floor in between your shoulders. Using one of your hands, roll the tennis ball away from you. Stay in plank position as you try to retrieve the ball.

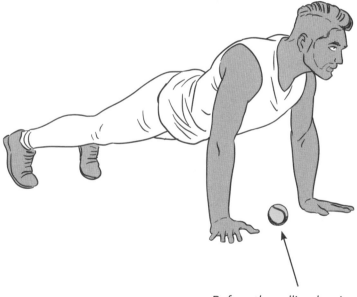

Before the rolling begins

DIY GYM: POST-WORKOUT MUSCLE-RELAXER

Release the tension in your muscles after a workout with a tennis ball instead of buying a foam roller. For your back, rest the ball in between your back and the floor (making sure it isn't directly on your spine) and roll it along the muscles by moving your body. Once you find a knot or tight area, keep the ball on this section of your back and relax your body, as if you were trying to touch the floor. Stay in this position for 2-4 minutes. It may feel uncomfortable but there's no gain without pain! (This is also the perfect exercise for those times when you have sat at a computer all day.)

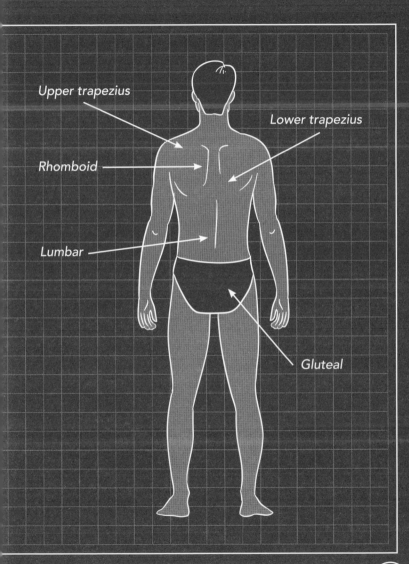

Upper trapezius

Lower trapezius

Rhomboid

Lumbar

Gluteal

EAT GINGER

If you feel like you've overworked yourself after your DIY gym session, make sure you increase the amount of ginger, fresh or powdered, in your diet by adding it to stir-fries, juices, smoothies or tea. It contains anti-inflammatory compounds and can reduce muscle soreness by 25 per cent if consumed daily. The ultimate power food!

Slice, dice or grate (or buy as powder from the supermarket!)

FOOD AND DRINK HACKS

Do you and your housemates argue over the best way to poach an egg? Do you wish you could cut down the time you spend in the kitchen but still have healthy meals? This chapter offers tips and tricks to put the fun back into cooking.

TACO-SHELL PLATE

To reduce your washing-up (and give you a delicious snack when you've finished your meal), use taco shells to serve your food instead of plates. If you don't have taco shells, make them using tortillas. Turn a muffin tray upside down and fit the tortillas in the gaps. Lightly spray them with cooking oil and cook for 10 minutes at 190°C.

A cupcake-tray-turned-tortilla-creator

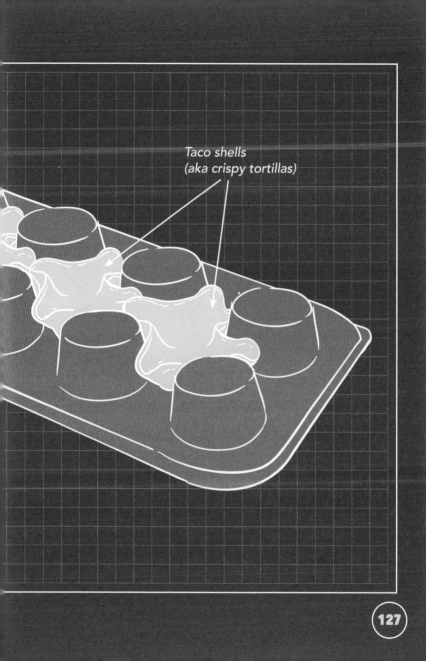

Taco shells
(aka crispy tortillas)

EASY PEELER

Whether it's a mango, avocado or kiwi, make peeling them easy with this hack, which requires just one glass. Slice your fruit of choice in half (removing the stone from the avo). Position your fruit so the point where the shell and the soft fruit meet is touching the edge of the glass. Then press down lightly and slide the fruit down so that the skin separates from it. If you foresee a terrible accident attempting this hack, maybe it's best to stick with a spoon.

Shell- and fruit-separating device

Don't slice your hand off in the process

EGGSHELL EXTRACTION

It's easy to end up dedicating more time than necessary to removing tiny bits of broken shell from a cracked egg. Especially when you've got more pressing things to do… like write an assignment.

Save time and your patience by wetting your finger before you attempt the extraction, and the water will act like a magnet to the shell.

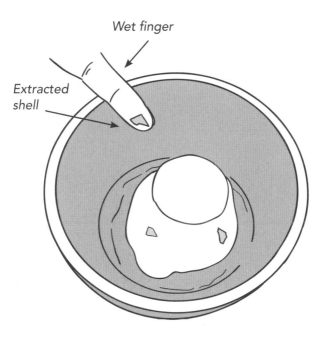

Wet finger

Extracted shell

MUG DESSERTS

Don't be a muggins – use a mug to whip up a delicious and cheap dessert that doesn't leave you with lots of washing-up.

Place 4 tbsp self-raising flour, 4 tbsp sugar, 1 egg, 3 tbsp cocoa powder, 3 tbsp chocolate spread, 3 tbsp milk and 3 tbsp vegetable oil in a large mug and mix with a fork until you create an even consistency. Heat it in the microwave on the highest setting for 1.5–3 minutes, depending on how powerful your microwave is (the best way to tell whether it is done is to keep checking every so often), then top with whipped cream and chocolate sauce for extra pleasure.

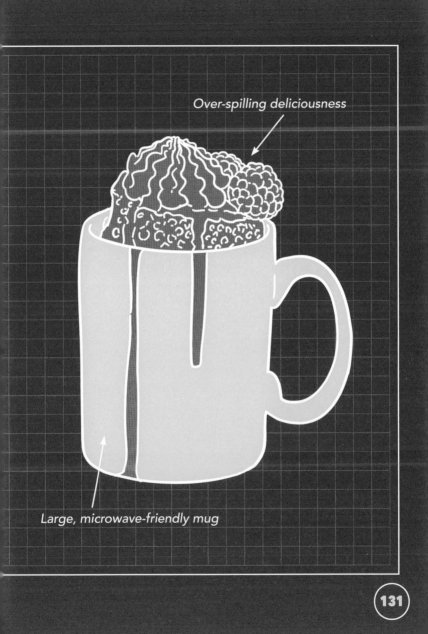

Over-spilling deliciousness

Large, microwave-friendly mug

DRYING HERBS

When you've splashed out your student loan on fresh herbs to make a special recipe, the leftover herbs can quickly turn limp and soggy. This hack will prevent your fresh herbs (and precious pennies) from going to waste.

First, pick off the leaves from the stalk and then place them on one half of a clean kitchen towel and cover with the other half of the towel. Microwave until dry – this should take around a minute, depending on the quantity – or until you can crumble them with your fingers. Grind them into a powder and decant into a labelled container or store whole. Add a sprinkle as you are cooking to make your meals more flavoursome and impress your culinary-inept friends.

Fresh leaves that need drying

Incredibly clean kitchen towel

CHEAP VACUUM SEALER

Sick of fresh fruit and veg going brown or soft too quickly? Try this hack to maximise their shelf life.

Transfer the fresh produce into a reusable sandwich bag and seal, leaving a gap big enough to fit a straw in. Place the straw in the bag and pinch the bag with your fingers either side of the straw. Suck the air out of the bag, remove the straw and seal the gap as quickly as you can. *Voilà*! You have your very own vacuum-sealed bag.

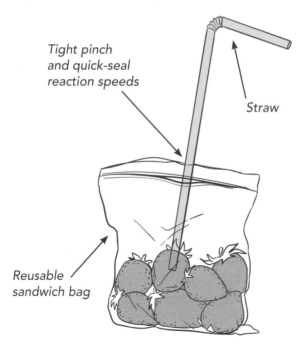

Tight pinch and quick-seal reaction speeds

Straw

Reusable sandwich bag

FRIED EGG MOULD

Getting an equal distribution of egg white when you fry an egg is tricky. Next time, use an onion ring – in order to separate an onion ring, slice a section of onion about 1 cm wide and remove the inner rings, leaving you with the biggest one – and pour the egg inside it. This will give you a perfectly round fried egg. To avoid waste, wrap the remaining onion in cling film and save it for your next meal – a cheese and onion omelette perhaps!

Textbook-perfect fried egg

Yummy onion rings

SAVE LEFTOVER WINE

If you have a little wine left over from the previous night and you don't think you can stomach the sight of it for at least another two days, freeze it to use in your cooking.

Remove the ice cube tray from the freezer and pour the remaining wine into the separate compartments, then put the tray back in the freezer, making sure it's stored completely flat (not just squashed in down the side of your oven chips). The wine cubes should last for up to three months, but be careful when removing them from the tray as wine will only partially freeze.

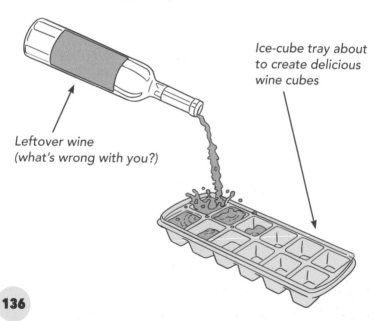

Ice-cube tray about to create delicious wine cubes

Leftover wine (what's wrong with you?)

YOGURT ICE LOLLIES

Frozen yogurt is the healthy alternative to ice cream and is sold in restaurants and supermarkets all over the country. But why buy an overpriced version when you can make your own cheaply and easily?

Buy a pack of yogurts and poke lollipop sticks through the lids of them. Then leave in the freezer for around 2 hours. Once solid, rip off the lid and remove the frozen yogurt from the pot to enjoy.

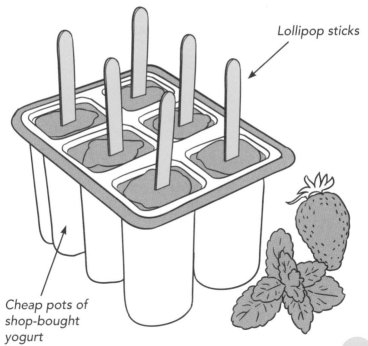

Lollipop sticks

Cheap pots of shop-bought yogurt

POACHING THE PERFECT EGG

Use this hack to impress your friends – everyone will be talking about it.

Add a drop of oil to the inside of a sandwich bag and rub the bag until the oil has covered it. Place the bag in a ramekin and crack an egg into it, then season with salt and pepper. Remove the bag from the ramekin and tie a knot in it close to the level of the egg, or secure with a bag clip. Place the bag in a pan of simmering water and cook for 3–4 minutes, depending on the size of the egg, then remove from the pan and cut underneath the knot with scissors. Serve the egg with some thickly buttered bread.

Not-yet-poached egg-in-a-bag

Pan of simmering water

PRESERVING YOUR SALAD LEAVES

Salad is a healthy side dish that requires minimal preparation, but when it's left to its own devices in the fridge it can quickly turn slimy and unappealing to eat, even if disguised with some dressing. To keep your leaves fresher for longer, try this simple hack.

Transfer the salad leaves into a plastic container with a lid, such as a Tupperware box. Then add a sheet of paper towel, close the lid and pop it in the fridge. Find the leaves a week later, having forgotten you even bought them, and be surprised that they are still in an edible state.

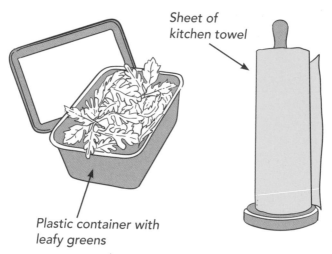

Sheet of kitchen towel

Plastic container with leafy greens

PIZZA SANDWICHES

Cold leftover pizza from the night before always seems yummier in principle than it actually tastes. Try jazzing it up next time with this effortless hack.

Cut off the crusts and save them (find out why on p.142), then place one pizza slice on top of another, both with the crusts facing outwards, so it looks like a sandwich. Add a splash of oil to a frying pan and heat. Place the sandwich in the pan and cook for a couple of minutes on each side. Once the cheese has turned into a gooey mess it is ready to enjoy.

Pizza that's soon going to resemble a sandwich

PIZZA-CRUST CROUTONS

Take the day-old pizza crusts that you didn't use making your ultimate pizza sandwich (see p.141) and cut into crouton-sized pieces with scissors. Add a splash of oil to a frying pan with some crushed garlic and heat until the garlic is golden. Then add the pizza croutons and stir so that they are coated with the oil and garlic. If there isn't enough oil, add more. Fry until the croutons are golden and crispy, then add a sprinkling of salt, pepper and fresh parsley and basil and fry for another minute. Serve with soup or a salad.

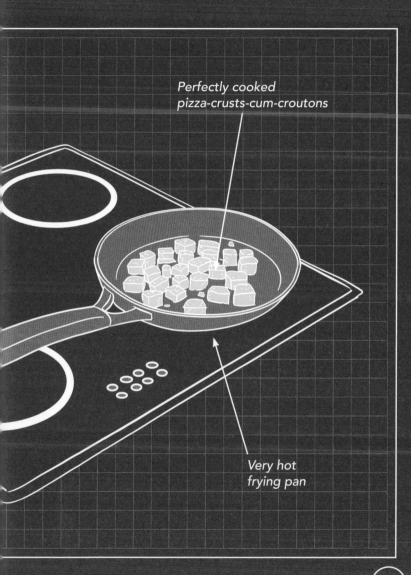

Perfectly cooked pizza-crusts-cum-croutons

Very hot frying pan

COFFEE BAG

You're a student – of course you can't afford a coffee-maker! But why miss out on your caffeine fix when you can create your own filter? All you need is some filter paper, ground coffee and string (make sure it doesn't contain plastic). Put the desired amount of coffee in the filter paper and then pinch the open ends together, twist it and secure by tying string around it. Make sure you leave enough string to be able to extract the coffee bag once it has brewed. Boil some water and follow the same steps as you'd take to make a cup of tea; then, once you think the coffee is strong enough, remove the coffee bag and add your optional extras, such as sugar and milk.

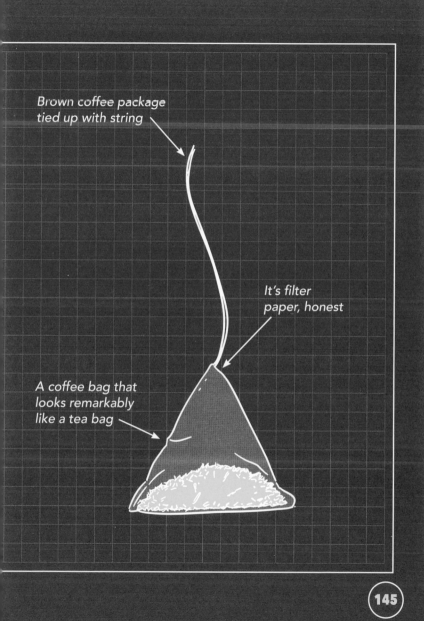

Brown coffee package tied up with string

It's filter paper, honest

A coffee bag that looks remarkably like a tea bag

COFFEE CUBES

Follow the instructions on how to make a coffee bag (p.144) to make enough coffee to fill an ice cube tray (one cup's worth should be enough). Once the coffee has been brewed, let it cool down to room temperature then pour it into the tray and freeze. When you're tempted to miss your early-morning class because you are too tired, grab yourself a cup of cold milk and add a few coffee cubes, depending on how strong you want it. Stir well and *voilà*, you have an iced coffee to go.

Either add a couple of cubes to the milk or the milk to the coffee cubes (how tired are you?)

MICROWAVE DOUGHNUT

If you have a meal that you want to reheat, put the food on a plate in the shape of doughnut (so there's a hole in the middle). This will ensure that the heat spreads evenly and you won't be surprised by an unexpected cold spot halfway through enjoying your dinner.

Leftovers arranged in a pretty circle

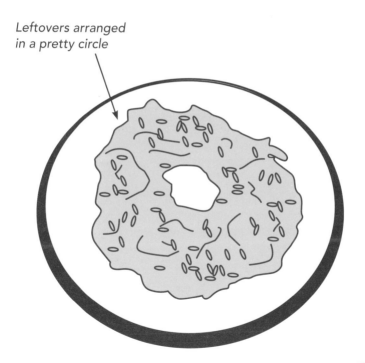

BULK COOKING

Supermarkets don't often cater for one, which is why you'll need to think wisely when it comes to buying your groceries, in order to keep waste to a minimum.

Plan the meals you want to eat for the week and buy more than you actually need. Then cook a giant-sized portion and separate the leftovers into plastic containers or foil trays with lids (sandwich bags and old margarine tubs are good too), which should be in abundance if you enjoy the odd takeaway. Allow the food to cool to room temperature, label the container(s) with the date the dish was made and pop it in the freezer. Food must be eaten within a month and must be thoroughly defrosted before reheating. NOTE: plastic containers and sandwich bags should not go in the oven when it comes to reheating your tasty meals.

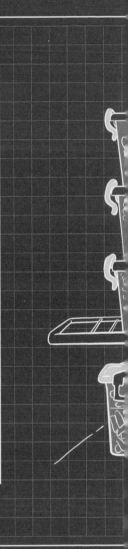

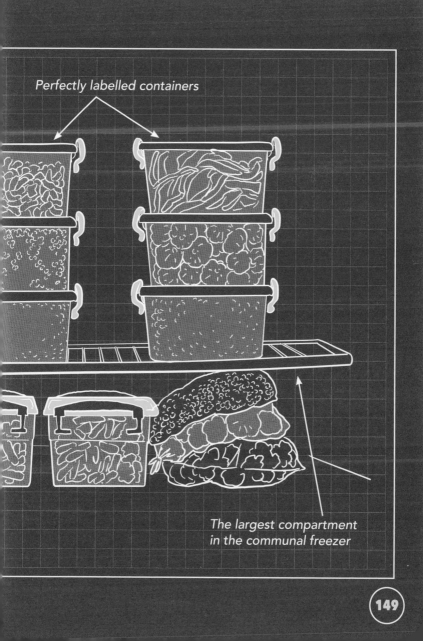

Perfectly labelled containers

The largest compartment in the communal freezer

PARTY HACKS

Are you hosting a party but don't know where to start with the preparation? Do you worry that you are spending too much of your money on booze? These hacks are guaranteed to promote you to being the host with the most, without having to splash the cash.

DIP HOLDERS

A party always means lots of washing-up. Reduce this as much as possible by using hollowed-out peppers to hold dips. When you're done with dip (usually within the first 5 minutes of people turning up) slice the peppers and enjoy eating your 'dishes'.

Where are the crisps?!

NEVER LOSE YOUR BOTTLE OPENER

Even when you think you've provided enough bottle openers at your party, you still end up searching endlessly for them. Make sure they never go AWOL again with this hack.

Find a bottle opener with a hole at the bottom of it and cut a relatively long strip of material or string and secure it to the bottle opener. Then attach the free end of string to somewhere easy to reach, such as a door or cupboard handle or the handle of your drinks bucket/cooler, if you're using one.

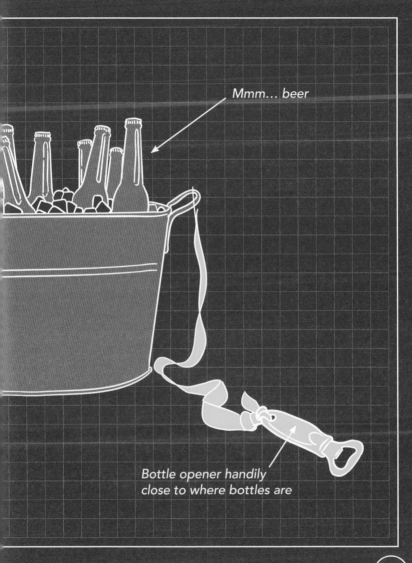

Mmm... beer

Bottle opener handily
close to where bottles are

WATER BALLOON ICE CUBES

You have your industrial-sized bottles of cheap booze and mixer ready but you want to chill them without the hassle of ice cubes. Find a big bucket or two and buy some water balloons. Fill the balloons with water and whack them in the freezer until solid. Then put them in the bucket with your bottles and, hey presto, you have an ice bucket that is non-spill – plus you can reuse the water balloons.

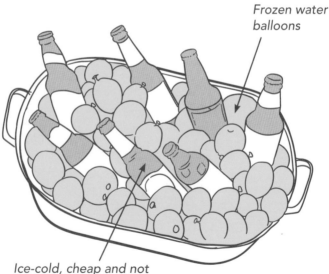

Frozen water balloons

Ice-cold, cheap and not very cheerful alcohol

CUP-CUM-JIGGER

Have you ever wondered why plastic red cups are ribbed? I have too. I still do to this day. And although I'm not aware of the official reason for their layered structure, I do know that they are great in situations where your hands need a little help to grip the cup (for instance, when you are having a dance-off with your friends – or strangers). Even more helpfully, though, they offer a rough guide of where to fill different types of alcohol up to when you're at a party. Instead of waking up the next morning not knowing how much you've had to drink, you'll be thanking these cups as you experience just a minor hangover due to your perfectly portioned-out drinks.

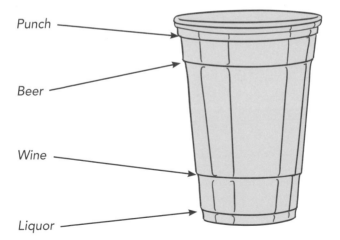

Punch

Beer

Wine

Liquor

CARD-FREE NIGHTS

You're at your most financially vulnerable when you've had a few to drink. You become friends with everyone and want to make sure they are having a good time by supplying them with constant top-ups. To make sure you wake up the morning after the night before without the sinking feeling in your stomach as you check your online banking, leave your wallet and cards at home and only take a budgeted amount of cash with you on your nights out.

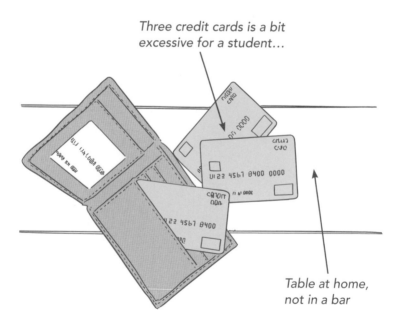

Three credit cards is a bit excessive for a student...

Table at home, not in a bar

BANK OF CHAP STICK

You've refrained from taking your wallet and cards out with you, but where to put the cash you carry? If you want to avoid being a target for pickpockets, use an empty chap stick to store it – no one will ever know it's there, unless of course you wave it about when you're at the bar.

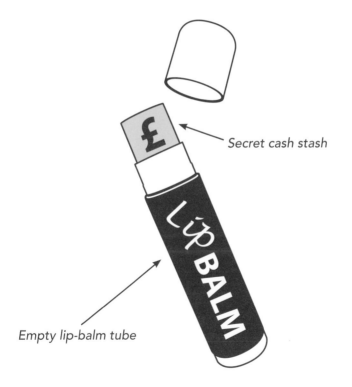

Secret cash stash

Empty lip-balm tube

ICE-CREAM CUTTER

Why faff around scooping when you can slice? (And why would any student have an ice-cream scoop lying around anyway?)

Remove the ice cream from its tub by turning it upside down and banging it lightly on a chopping board. Then, with a sharp knife, simply cut the ice cream into individual slices for your guests. If there's any left (unlikely!), wrap the remainder in cling film and put it back in the freezer.

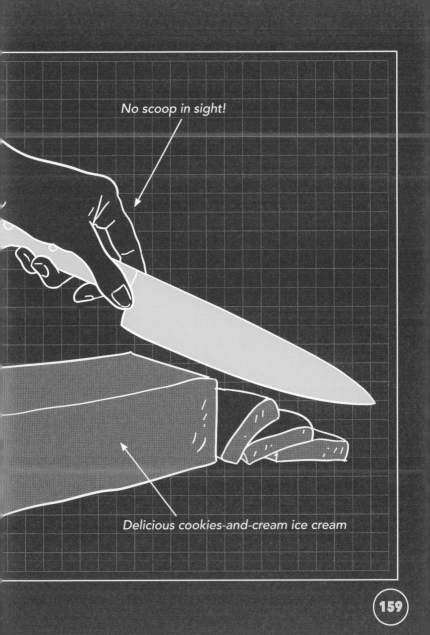

No scoop in sight!

Delicious cookies-and-cream ice cream

LIGHT-UP BALLOONS

This hack will take your standard balloons to the next stage of awesomeness – the only additional items you need are glow sticks (especially fitting if you're having a UV theme).

Just before your party, activate the glow sticks by bending them. Blow up each balloon just over its natural inflated size. While pinching the end of the balloon, take the glow stick and feed it into the balloon so it's fully inside. Tie a knot in the balloon. Arrange the balloons nicely and dim the lights when your guests arrive, then get that party started.

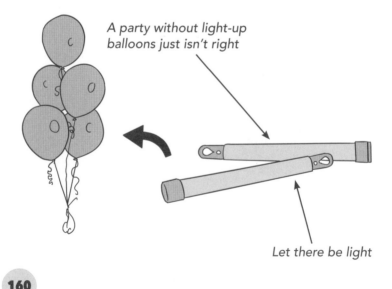

A party without light-up balloons just isn't right

Let there be light

CHEAP VODKA FILTERER

You hate the taste of cheaply made vodka but there's no way you're going to fork out for anything more. And there's no need to with this hack, as it will make all your good-tasting-vodka dreams come true. Simply decant the dirty, dirty vodka into a filter jug and pour it out again into a clean jug. Repeat the filtering process a couple of times. Make sure this filter jug now remains for vodka only, as the taste of the spirit might still cling to it.

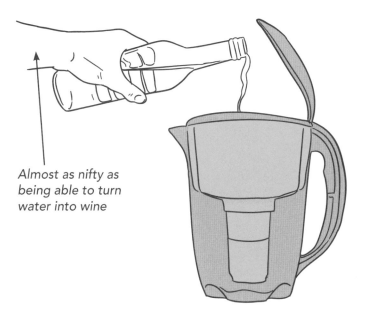

Almost as nifty as being able to turn water into wine

CUP TRACKER

To prevent piles and piles of washing-up after your party or pre-drinks, give your guests glasses with labels or tags attached to them with their names on. This helps guests locate their cups instead of grabbing a new one each time. Add some humour to the situation by writing down their nicknames. The guests who don't know each other will soon get chatting as they are overcome with curiosity.

Misspelled name that the host will get grief for

Tags or stickers to write the misspelled names on

PLASTIC CUP LANTERNS

Make the area where you are hosting a delight to the eye with this simple hack. Grab yourself a string of LED lights and some cheap transparent plastic cups – the number of cups you need will depend on the number of lights there are. Then cut small Xs into the bottoms of the cups and push the lights through them. Find a good place to hang them and let them literally light up the party.

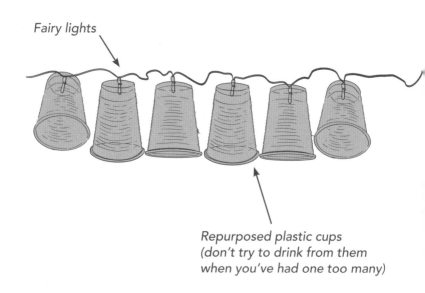

Fairy lights

*Repurposed plastic cups
(don't try to drink from them
when you've had one too many)*

CAKE ICING STENCIL

Is it a friend's birthday soon, but you're no cake-decorating artist? Personalised cakes can be super-expensive for budgeting students to think about giving to a friend, so try this hack to cut the cost and create your own instead.

Buy a pre-iced cake from the supermarket and stencil your special message into the icing with a toothpick – this allows you to see your design and check it's perfect before moving on to the next step. Then trace the outline with the icing colour of your choice, and you'll have a perfect, professional-looking personalised cake in no time.

The writing is on the cake (promise!)

Voila!

HANGOVER HACKS

Do you wish there was a miracle cure for the world's worst hangover? Unfortunately this chapter can't offer miracles but it can help ease the pain with the following tips and tricks.

WATER ME

One of the main causes of a hangover is dehydration, so try to pump some water into your body as quickly as possible. Eat lots of water-rich fruit and vegetables, such as watermelon, papaya, cucumber and celery, as studies suggest that they work twice as effectively as simply drinking water due to the high levels of hydrating minerals, sugars and salts that are present as well.

*Nutrient-providing,
water-retaining watermelon*

STOMACH LINER

Try to prevent your hangover symptoms as much as possible with this hack (ironically you need to have a hardened stomach to cope). Before you start drinking, guzzle down a shot of olive oil. The grease helps to line the stomach walls and slow down the absorption of alcohol, which means you should wake up feeling less like death personified.

A posh-looking shot of olive oil for the purposes of an aesthetically pleasing book

REVITALISING MAGIC

Studies suggest that honey is good for hangovers because it contains fructose, which helps speed up the breakdown of the alcohol. Lemon is said to speed up recovery time as it has alkaline properties, which help restore pH levels in the body. So while you're having a pint of water the day after, try warming it up and adding some honey and a slice of lemon to it.

A drizzle of honey

Some lemon-infused tea

SLEEP PERMIT

Sleeping as much as possible the day after drinking will help you feel better (and that's not just because you aren't awake). Although we tend to 'crash' when we've had too much to drink, our actual sleep is disrupted by our body's attempts to break down the alcohol. This is our official licence to chill! If you need to study or revise the following day, then chilling isn't an option – and drinking the day before isn't either!

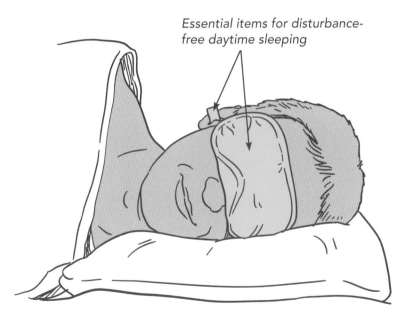

Essential items for disturbance-free daytime sleeping

HEADACHE RELIEF

When you wake up with a pounding head, it sometimes feels like life isn't worth living. But then you realise you have an assignment deadline for the following day and you haven't done any work for it. Life definitely isn't worth living but somehow you have to suck it up and keep going. To try to relieve the tension building up in your head (where thoughts and ideas should be continually flowing by now), try soaking a flannel in cold water, wringing it out, and holding it on your forehead for immediate pain relief.

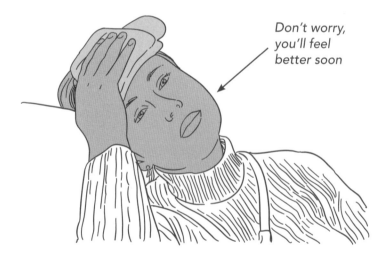

Don't worry, you'll feel better soon

HEADACHE RELIEF 2

If the flannel on the head hasn't helped, try doing a headstand against a wall for a couple of minutes. It may seem like the last thing you want to do when suffering from a hangover but being upside-down helps to stimulate the mind and cleanse the liver and kidneys. There is a method to the madness after all!

Picture-perfect headstand

Soft mat for extra padding

EXERCISE YOURSELF BETTER

Exercise can help you feel better when you have a hangover as it releases feel-good endorphins. The sweating-it-out theory isn't scientifically true, but moderate physical activity such as a brisk walk or a bike ride (that's if you're not still over the limit) after lots of water and some food can help elevate your mood. The fresh air does wonders too.

MISCELLANEOUS HACKS

If you couldn't find the hack you were looking for in the previous chapters, perhaps you'll have better luck finding it here. In this chapter you will find hacks that are so weird and wacky that we had to create a whole new chapter for them. From creating a festive boozy advent calendar to personalising your clock to display your daily planner, these hacks are the final steps to becoming a student-hack maestro!

CHEESY FEET PREVENTER

If you notice that your feet are starting to pong a bit, insert crumpled up pieces of newspaper into the accused shoes to help absorb the smell. Just make sure you have finished the crossword before trying out this hack.

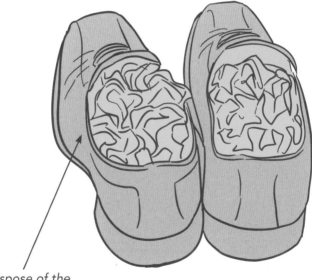

Dispose of the newspaper once finished (yuck!)

BOOZY ADVENT CALENDAR

Make the best advent calendar yet with just a crate of beer and a marker pen! You'll be ho-ho-hoing all the way to Christmas Day – although if you have assignments to finish, it's best to complete those first!

How convenient that there are 24 bottles in a crate!

BLACKBOARD NOTEPAD

Make your to-do lists even more visible to the eye by sticking mini blackboards (available at most craft stores) onto the fronts of your notebooks with glue. Ensure each to-do list corresponds with the notebook you use for each of your modules. Every time you have a lecture, you will be reminded of forthcoming homework, assignments and exams when you take your notebook out of your bag.

English:
Do homework
Start essay

Now there's no excuse not to miss an important study date

CLOCK ORGANISER

Make time management easier by turning your cheap, plain old clock into a planning device. Separate the front glass section from the face of the clock and grab some colouring pens. Fill in the relevant sections of the clockface with different colours and create a key on a bit of paper or mini whiteboard to show which colour represents which activity. Assemble the clock and hang it over your desk, so you'll always be able to see what you should be doing at that particular time.

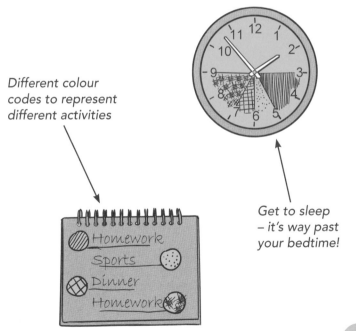

Different colour codes to represent different activities

Get to sleep – it's way past your bedtime!

DIY FACE TONER

When times are tough and you don't have the money to keep forking out on expensive beauty products, try this hack to create a face toner that's just as good as the leading brands. After you wash your face, apply a solution of 1 tbsp apple cider vinegar – available from supermarkets and health shops – and 2 cups of water to your skin and let it dry without washing it off. It beats buying cheap products that'll bring you out in spots the following morning!

Your skin will feel tighter, smoother and cleaner

TEETH WHITENER

Why use charcoal when you can use a banana peel?! Rub the outside of the skin on your top and bottom teeth for about a minute, leave for 10 minutes, then brush your teeth as you usually would. Do this a few times a week and reap the benefits.

Who would have thought it?!

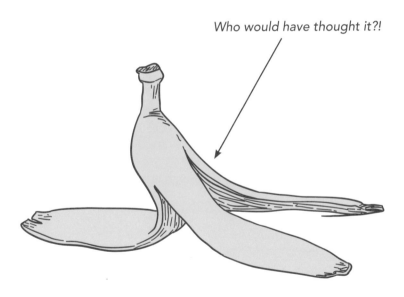

NON-TOXIC ANT REPELLENT

The sun is out and you've planned a picnic – perhaps to celebrate that you've successfully written all your assignments, got through the year in an ultra-organised manner and breezed through your exams, thanks to all the new student hacks in your life. Although they didn't get an invitation, an army of ants has joined too, with the aim of sabotaging your day. Stop them in their tracks with this ant repellent you so niftily created and packed in your bag just before you left the house.

Pour equal amounts of water and white vinegar into a spray bottle and mix, then liberally apply the solution to the area where you'll be sitting. Now you are free to enjoy your well-deserved picnic in pest-free peace.

Homemade solution to solve all ant-fuelled picnic problems

FINAL WORD

Congratulations – you are now a Student Hack hero. Whatever life throws at you, you can handle it – whether it's multiple deadlines or a deadly hangover. Feel free to pass on these little nuggets of genius to all you meet and plugging the book wouldn't hurt. (I've still got to eat – I haven't found a hack for this yet.)

If you have some student hacks that are not featured in this book and you think they deserve to be in print, email them to auntie@summersdale.com.

Until next time – get hacking!

HACKS INDEX

STUDY AND EXAM HACKS

HEALTH AND WELL-BEING HACKS

IMAGE CREDITS

p.3: © Nigel French/Shutterstock.com; LOVEgraphic/Shutterstock.com; Sim Va/Shutterstock.com

p.6: © Coprid; LunaseeStudios; John Seo; buhai_adeus; Africa Studio; grmarc; aradaphotography; MyImages - Micha; Charlie Edwards; HomeStudio; LightField Studios; Sashkin; Aleksandr Bryliaev; Sony Ho; Juriah Mosin; Kamira; Ranoris/Shutterstock.com

p.9: © Nigel French/Shutterstock.com; LOVEgraphic/Shutterstock.com; Sim Va/Shutterstock.com

p.11: © Lemberg Vector studio/Shutterstock.com

p.13: © Luisa Leal Photography/Shutterstock.com

p.14: © stockphoto-graf/Shutterstock.com

p.15: © Shutterstock.com

p.17: © Sergiy Kuzmin/Shutterstock.com

p.18: © Chea01/Shutterstock.com; Filip Miletic/Shutterstock.com; onsuda/Shutterstock.com

p.19: © Jasminko Ibrakovic/Shutterstock.com; GzP_Design/Shutterstock.com

p.23: © Roman Samokhin/Shutterstock.com; Mindscape studio/Shutterstock.com; Vlue/Shutterstock.com

p.24: © Seregam/Shutterstock.com; Tracy Burge/Shutterstock.com; Jake Rennaker/Shutterstock.com

p.25: © Sirastock/Shutterstock.com; Pavel Vinnik/Shutterstock.com; MagicDogWorkshop/Shutterstock.com

p.27: © Nils Z/Shutterstock.com; Konstantin Faraktinov/Shutterstock.com

p.29: © Macrovector/Shutterstock.com

p.30: © HomeStudio/Shutterstock.com

p.31: © Africa Studio/Shutterstock.com

p.33: © g_tech/Shutterstock.com

p.34: © Monkey Business Images/Shutterstock.com

p.35: © Paul.J.West/Shutterstock.com

p.39: © Julia Karo/Shutterstock.com; Yulia Mozes/Shutterstock.com; kmarfu/Shutterstock.com

p.41: © Aleksandr Bryliaev/Shutterstock.com; Sony Ho/Shutterstock.com

p.43: © BrAt82/Shutterstock.com; John T Takai/Shutterstock.com

p.44: © Konstantin Gushcha/Shutterstock.com

p.45: © focal point/Shutterstock.com; Mile Atanasov/Shutterstock.com

p.47: © Salman Timur/Shutterstock.com

p.48: © s-ts/Shutterstock.com

p.49: © Stock Up/Shutterstock.com; Levent Konuk/Shutterstock.com

p.51: © Kostsov/Shutterstock.com; Stocksnapper/Shutterstock.com

p.52: © Africa Studio/Shutterstock.com

p.53: © casadaphoto/Shutterstock.com; mind5563/Shutterstock.com; Paul Michael Hughes/Shutterstock.com

p.54: © Guzel Studio/Shutterstock.com; ideatraveller/Shutterstock.com

p.55: © buhai_adeus/Shutterstock.com

p.57: © Freedom_Studio/Shutterstock.com; Olga Kovalenko/Shutterstock.com; relish5/Shutterstock.com; Kitch Bain/Shutterstock.com

p.58: © cord image: Freedom_Studio/Shutterstock.com; Pumidol/Shutterstock.com

p.59: © s_karau/Shutterstock.com

p.62: © Anna Efimova/Shutterstock.com; urfin/Shutterstock.com

p.63: © xiaorui/Shutterstock.com; vvoe/Shutterstock.com; Surrphoto/Shutterstock.com

p.66: © sirtravelalot/Shutterstock.com

If you're interested in finding out more about
our books, find us on Facebook at
Summersdale Publishers
and follow us on Twitter at
@Summersdale.

WWW.SUMMERSDALE.COM